THE COLLECTED WORKS

OF

C. G. JUNG

SUPPLEMENTARY VOLUME A

ORIGINAL EDITORS

SIR HERBERT READ

MICHAEL FORDHAM, M.D., M.R.C.P.

GERHARD ADLER, PH.D.

Editor of Volume A:

WILLIAM MC GUIRE

THE
ZOFINGIA
LECTURES

C. G. JUNG

TRANSLATED BY JAN VAN HEURCK

WITH AN INTRODUCTION BY MARIE-LOUISE VON FRANZ

ROUTLEDGE & KEGAN PAUL
LONDON, MELBOURNE AND HENLEY

FIRST PUBLISHED IN GREAT BRITAIN IN 1983
BY ROUTLEDGE & KEGAN PAUL PLC
39 STORE STREET, LONDON WC1E 7DD,
296 BEACONSFIELD PARADE, MIDDLE PARK, MELBOURNE 3206, AUSTRALIA
AND BROADWAY HOUSE, NEWTON ROAD, HENLEY-ON-THAMES,
OXON RG9 1EN

THIS EDITION IS BEING PUBLISHED IN ENGLAND
BY ROUTLEDGE & KEGAN PAUL PLC, AND IN THE
UNITED STATES OF AMERICA FOR BOLLINGEN
FOUNDATION BY PRINCETON UNIVERSITY PRESS.
THIS IS SUPPLEMENTARY VOLUME A OF THE COL-
LECTED WORKS

ISBN 0-7100-9947-9
PRINTED IN THE UNITED STATES OF AMERICA

EDITORIAL NOTE

Jung was admitted to the medical school of Basel University on April 18, 1895, two months before his twentieth birthday. On May 18, he became a member of the Basel section of the Zofingiaverein, a Swiss student fraternity with members in several universities.[1] The club's program included lectures and serious or mock-serious discussions at its weekly meetings, as well as beer-drinking parties, outings, and dances. Jung's father, who also had been a Zofingia member,[2] died on January 28, 1896; and, according to Gustav Steiner, another Zofingia comrade,[3] Jung did not participate in discussions at the weekly club meetings until after he had given his first lecture, in November 1896. Thereafter Jung gave four lectures, including his inaugural address upon becoming chairman of the Basel club during the winter semester of 1897/98.

After Jung completed his medical studies, in July 1900, it would appear that he packed away the manuscripts of his Zofingia lectures and, as with the letters that Freud was later to write him, gave little thought to them for a great many years. No allusions to his Zofingia experiences are to be found in his scientific writings or published letters. There is nothing about them among the recollections he brought forth in the 1925 Seminar, nor in the subsequent seminars. Only in 1935 were some vivid particulars of Jung's Zofingia involvement published, not from his pen but from that of his old friend and fellow alumnus Albert Oeri, in a Festschrift for Jung's

---

[1] Henri Ellenberger, *The Discovery of the Unconscious* (New York, 1970), p. 665, citing Gustav Steiner, "Erinnerungen an Carl Gustav Jung," *Basler Stadtbuch*, 1965, pp. 117-63.

[2] *Memories, Dreams, Reflections by C. G. Jung*, ed. Aniela Jaffé (New York and London, 1963), p. 95/99. (Page citations differ in the two editions.)

[3] Steiner's memoir was based on research in the protocols of the Zofingiaverein.

sixtieth birthday.[4] In the chapter "Student Years" in *Memories, Dreams, Reflections,* Jung alluded to his fraternity life without mentioning the Zofingia by name. A fuller account of the Zofingia episode, based principally on the memoir by Gustav Steiner, was published in 1970 by Henri Ellenberger.[5] That Jung had preserved his hand-written lectures of the 1890s was not generally known.

Jung's Zofingia manuscripts first came to public notice when his heirs made them available, along with other documents and pictorial matter, for a memorial exhibition marking the centenary of Jung's birth. He would have been one hundred years old on July 26, 1975. Under the auspices of the city of Zurich, the C. G. Jung Institute, and the Psychological Club of Zurich, the exhibition, including much original material, was shown in March-April 1975 at the Helmhaus in Zurich and later in Basel and Bern. Some pages of the Zofingia manuscripts and photographs of Jung in club regalia were included.[6]

When, in March 1975, Aniela Jaffé called my attention to the Zofingia items in the Helmhaus exhibition, I inquired of Franz Jung, Professor Jung's son, about the possibility of considering the lectures for publication. He subsequently sent a photocopy of the manuscripts, and we sought the advice of the editors of the Collected Works, Gerhard Adler and Michael Fordham, and of two other advisers, Professor Ernst Benz and Professor Walter Kaufmann. On their recommendation, the publication of the Zofingia Lectures was approved by Princeton University Press as a supplement to the Collected Works. The Jung family supervised the preparation and careful checking of a typewritten transcript of the manuscripts, from which the present translation was made.

The translator, Jan van Heurck, had the advice of Krishna Winston, Dorothee Schneider, and Marie-Louise von Franz. The annotation is the work of Miss van Heurck in collaboration with the

---

[4] "Ein paar Erinnerungen," in *Die kulturelle Bedeutung der komplexen Psychologie,* ed. the Psychological Club, Zurich (Berlin, 1935), pp. 524-28; tr. Lisa Ress, "Some Youthful Memories," in *C. G. Jung Speaking,* ed. William McGuire and R.F.C. Hull (Princeton and London, 1977), pp. 3-10.

[5] Ellenberger, *Discovery of the Unconscious,* pp. 665-66, 687-88.

[6] Subsequently the Pro Helvetia Foundation sponsored a photographic display on large panels, based on the Helmhaus exhibition; this was shown widely in Europe and America. The exhibitions formed the basis of a book edited by Aniela Jaffé: C. G. Jung, *Bild und Wort* (Zurich: Walter Verlag, 1977), tr. Krishna Winston, *C. G. Jung: Word and Image* (Princeton, 1979).

editor. Some notes by Miss Schneider and Dr. von Franz carry their initials. Original sources of Jung's quotations are cited where available. Unless otherwise indicated, the translations of quotations are by Jan van Heurck.

The more significant or interesting of Jung's manuscript deletions, interpolations, and marginalia are indicated in the footnotes. There are no editorial deletions from what Jung evidently intended as his final lecture text.

*

Acknowledgment is gratefully made to the following persons for advice, information, and other assistance: Dr. Gerhard Adler, Mr. Georg Duthaler, Professor Manfred Halpern, Mrs. Aniela Jaffé, Mr. Franz Jung, Mrs. Lilly Jung-Merker, Professor Carl Schorske, Dr. A. Joshua Sherman, the Staatsarchiv des Kantons Basel-Stadt (Dr. Andreas Staehelin and Dr. Ulrich Barth), and Professor Theodore Ziolkowski.

W. M.

TABLE OF CONTENTS

CONTENTS

LIST OF ILLUSTRATIONS

INTRODUCTION

Although I believe that Jung himself would not have cared to publish these juvenilia, they are highly interesting, readable, and important. They are lectures he gave to his fellow students at Basel University when he was between twenty-one and twenty-three years of age. On the 18th of May 1895 he had joined the Basel section of the color-wearing fraternity "Zofingia," in which it was a tradition for the members to give, from time to time, lectures about their special fields of interest. The lectures were supposed to meet a high scientific standard and at the same time to express political and other opinions in an outspoken manner befitting a closed circle whose members felt free of academic and social conventions. The reader has to bear this in mind when reading the often sarcastic and strong language that the young medical candidate, C. G. Jung, used in expressing his convictions.

It is a great advantage that the lectures Jung gave at the Zofingia may now be published (by permission of the Jung family, in whose possession they are preserved), because what we had known about them only from the recollections of Gustav Steiner, a co-member of the Zofingia, had given rise to misunderstandings. Steiner commented on *Memories, Dreams, Reflections*, upon its publication after Jung's death.[1] Jung himself had a double reaction toward his experiences in the Zofingia: his student days were "a good time," he wrote,[2] and a source of friendship and intellectual exchange, but he also said how lonely he really was, because his fellow students failed to understand what he wanted to say. To them he was full of exuberant, aggressive, youthful élan. They had little idea of how much he suffered because, although they were duly impressed by his lectures, they obviously did not really take them as seriously as Jung hoped they would. If one looks back today at what two wars and a general cultural decay have led to, one can better understand

---

[1] "Erinnerungen an Carl Gustav Jung," *Basler Stadtbuch*, 1965, pp. 117-63.
[2] *Memories, Dreams, Reflections*, ed. Aniela Jaffé (New York and London, 1963), p. 97/101.

the aggressive urgency of his talks.[3] Steiner himself states that the students then lived in a purely materialist "sleepy" time which had nothing to offer to young people. "We then experienced the catastrophe."[4] Jung, seeing that catastrophe, the First World War, coming, was impelled to warn them urgently. It disappointed him how little his companions reacted to it. As a whole, however, the Zofingia was for Jung a positive experience. When he joined, its Basel section had 120 members, 80 of whom were active. They often met in smaller circles devoted to special interests, which Jung did not join, and, as his friend Albert Oeri tells us, he did not much care for the parties devoted to drinking and dancing.[5] Yet, in his paper, Oeri draws a lively, sympathetic picture of his young friend. He was a cheerful comrade, "always prepared to revolt against the 'League of Virtue.' " He later discovered that he could dance quite well without having learned to. His student name, incidentally, was *Walze* (barrel).

Jung was active mainly in the scientific discussions. In spite of being an outsider in his views, he dominated and fascinated his audience, "luring them into speculative areas of thought which to the majority of us were an alien wonderland. . . . It was wonderful to let oneself be lectured to, as one sat with him in his room. His little dachshund would look at me so earnestly, just as though he understood every word, and Jung did not fail to tell me how the sensitive animal would sometimes whimper piteously when occult forces were active." Often they sat until late in the night at the pub called "Breo." Jung did not like to walk home alone through the Nightingale Wood, so he told his friend such interesting stories

[3] How Steiner himself still later took Jung's polemics as a "pleasure" and an "exercise" of discussion can be read in his article (p. 141, for instance). One alleged contradiction pointed out by Steiner has been taken over by Henri Ellenberger (*The Discovery of the Unconscious*, New York, 1970, p. 688), namely, that Jung in a discussion asserted that the theological axiom according to which God can be experienced is wrong, that he himself "never had such an experience." Steiner (p. 161) sees in this a contradiction to Jung's experience of God which he relates in *Memories, Dreams, Reflections*. What he overlooks is that Jung meant that the axiomatic "good God" of the theologians cannot be experienced. What we have are experiences that are mediated by or possibly spring from the unconscious and that are often very "strange." Steiner and Ellenberger missed the point in this respect.

[4] Steiner, "Erinnerungen," p. 161.

[5] See Albert Oeri, "Some Youthful Memories," in *C. G. Jung Speaking*, ed. W. McGuire and R.F.C. Hull (Princeton and London, 1977), p. 7. (Orig. 1935.)

that he came along with him without noticing it. When he stayed out until it was already morning, Jung picked some flowers to soften his mother's anger.

In the Zofingia Jung kept silent in the meetings for the first three semesters, but later took a leading role.

The motto of the Zofingia was *Patriae, amicitiae, litteris* ("For fatherland, friendship, and literature"). The fraternity had been founded in 1820/21, more or less simultaneously with the German *Burschenschaften*, at first in sympathy with the latter but also, almost at once, in opposition to them, because the Germans wanted to integrate and absorb the Swiss into a pan-Germanic movement. But from the beginning, the Zofingia stressed its purely Swiss independence.[6] It was the time after the Napoleonic Wars, when the survivors of the pre-Napoleonic era sought everywhere to abolish the republican order Napoleon had instituted. The German student movement was, at that time, a romantic uprising characterized by patriotism and liberal ideals, fighting against all shades of absolutism, the prerogatives of certain classes, and (mostly in Switzerland) the rule of the urban aristocracy over the country folk. Although in a moderate way revolutionary, the Swiss movement firmly upheld the idea of a legal state, with the Swiss army as a means to defend the independence and neutrality of the nation. However, events brought a split into the fraternity, and the more conservative group collided with the more liberal. The latter even founded a separate fraternity called "Helvetia" or, in the thirties, "Neo-Zofingia." The split lasted until 1856, when the two groups were reunited as a new Zofingia, the society which Jung joined. From his approval of the Langenthal episode, a quarrel between liberal and conservative students in which the liberals won, we can see that his feelings were not with the more conservative but with the liberal[7] tendencies within the reunited fraternity. For this reunion, however, the Zofingia paid a price: from then on its members no longer identified with actual party politics but set up the ideal of supporting patriotism, friendship, and education only in a general way, leaving each member to join any party he liked

---

[6] For this and the following see Werner Kundert, *Abriss der Geschichte des Schweizerischen Zofingervereins* (Lausanne, 1961). I owe the knowledge of this book and other information to the kindness of Kaspar Birkhäuser.

[7] "Liberal" is meant here not as a party identification but in the sense of supporting individual and general freedom (free of social classes).

(except the anarchists or other parties which worked for the overthrow of the Swiss state and its independence).[8] Although this saved the unity of the organization, it also led to the perils against which Jung seems to warn in his presidential address, namely that the fraternity was in danger of becoming a peaceful, "sleepy," young men's club with no more spirit to fight for realistic goals. But viewed as a whole, Jung's relationship to the Zofingia was positive, because the fraternity helped him step out of his isolation and formulate the ideas churning in him at that stage of his life.

What makes these early ideas so interesting is that they not only show where Jung stood at that point, but also how consistent his views of that youthful time are with his later thought and which questions tortured him at that time—questions for which he found answers in later life.

In his first lecture, "The Border Zones of Exact Science" (November 1896), he begins with a vehement attack on the inertia, stupidity, and conventionality of most scientists and exposes contemporary materialistic society as a giant with feet of clay. Although the views of physics that he criticizes are naturally outdated, it is fascinating to see how Jung attacks just the weak points.

First he shows the absurdity of the concept of ether, which was generally believed in then, until Albert Einstein showed, through his theory of relativity, that it is an unnecessary hypothesis. The second problem that Jung raises is the explanation of gravitation, to which he wrongly attributed some "metaphysical" quality. Science has since then advanced in its exploration, but it may be noted that gravitation is still the one force which on account of its extreme weakness cannot yet be included in a unified field theory, and its relativization in psychokinesis is still a matter of discussion.[9] Jung's instinct thus went directly to certain weak points in the coarsely materialistic physical theories of his time, and although his thesis— seen from the point of view of today's knowledge—is outdated, modern physics has certainly not yet solved the riddles he touched upon.[10]

---

[8] Article 2, in Kundert, *Abriss*, p. 22.

[9] A survey of current discussion is presented by E. Bauer and W. von Lucadou, "Methoden und Ergebnisse der Psychokinese-Forschung," in *Die Psychologie des 20. Jahrhunderts*, xv (1979), pp. 494ff.

[10] Cf. H. Schopper, "Die jüngste Entwicklung der Bilder von der Grundstruktur der Materie," *Naturwissenschaften*, 68 (1981), 307-313. I owe the knowledge of this

Jung's further attack is turned against the concept of a mechanical generation of life out of inorganic, i.e., "dead," matter. The vitalistic standpoint with which he sympathizes lost the battle in subsequent years, but today we approach a turning point again, where scientists begin to reconsider the possibility that acausal creative processes (synchronicity or "self-organization" by a spiritual agency) may lie at the beginning of life.[11] If we can believe R. Ruyer's report, in *La Gnose de Princeton*,[12] there are even leading physicists, especially in the United States, who believe in "mind over matter" in a way which Jung himself—in my opinion—would judge as too one-sidedly spiritualistic.

It is remarkable how Jung at that time, when the rise of materialism in science had only begun, saw its weak points. But what has he in mind as an alternative? He speaks only at the end of his lecture of two "metaphysical principles" postulated by the mystery of gravitation and of the origin of life, two phenomena which, as he says, "are virtually a closed book." He means by this the possibility that an immaterial phenomenon might manifest materially, but he does not explain this further. The first lecture stops short here with the criticism of materialism as "intellectual death" and only opens the door for what he really wants to say in his second lecture. Thus the first lecture must be understood as a deliberate preparation of the way for showing what he had in mind, which— he knew well—would be shocking for his audience.

The second lecture is entitled "Some Thoughts on Psychology" (May 1897). It opens with a quotation from Kant which emphasizes that morality is essential in science and that all philosophical investigations into concepts of God and of "the other world" would be worthless without morality. This brings in an important point, to which I will return only later. The text then continues with quotations from David Strauss, Schopenhauer, and Kant, stressing

exposé to the kindness of Dr. Wilhelm Just. Cf. also the excellent survey "Parapsychologie und Physik," by W. von Lucadou and K. Kornwachs, in *Der Psychologie des 20. Jahrhunderts*, xv (1975) pp. 581ff.

[11] Cf. Wolfgang Pauli, "Naturwissenschaftliche und erkenntnistheoretische Aspekte der Ideen vom Unbewussten," in *Aufsätze und Vorträge über Physik und Erkenntnistheorie* (Brunswick, 1961), pp. 123f. And today: Erich Jantsch and C. H. Waddington, *Evolution and Consciousness* (Reading, Mass., 1976), esp. pp. 49f. Cf. also E. Jantsch, *Die Selbstorganisation des Universums* (Darmstadt, 1979) *passim*, and Bernard d'Espagnat, *A la recherche du réel* (Paris, 1979).

[12] Paris, 1974.

the existence of "spirits" or "immaterial natures" beyond the bodies, and of "another world" with which our soul is linked already during our lifetime. Then Jung adds to these quotations the idea of the existence of a nonphysiological "intellectual being" or "life force" which some contemporary vitalistic physiologists also postulated. This life-principle, i.e., the soul, he says, "extends far beyond our consciousness"—here Jung first mentions indirectly the idea of an unconscious psyche. This soul is intelligent (purposeful in its acts) and independent of space-time.[13] These three aspects of the psyche are concepts that Jung retained throughout his life. To validate this view Jung then brings in a wealth of spiritualistic documentation about materialization phenomena, telekinesis, the "double," telepathy, clairvoyance, prophetic dreams, etc. We can see how the "reality of the psyche"—this basic concept of later Jungian psychology—is understood at that time and find in it also the background for Jung's dissertation, "On the Psychology and Pathology of So-Called Occult Phenomena."[14]

At the end of his lecture Jung returns to his first point: the need to bring morality back into science as a counterforce against the materialism that "poisons our morality and induces the moral instability of the educated classes." He specially mentions experiments involving "the cruel torture of animals which is a mockery of all human decency. . . . No truth obtained by unethical means has the moral right to exist." This point, which I want to stress, has not won out in our time. The immorality of science has only increased since then. The widespread opposition nowadays against atomic plants and against vivisection is still belittled as "unreasonable" and "unscientific," just as if a moral or feeling reaction had no right to exist.

Then follows, in Jung's lecture, an attack against the representatives of religion and their ineffectualness, because they deny themselves what for Jung is the very essence of religion: the reality of *mystery* and of the "extrasensory realm." Here again we meet a point of view that Jung never gave up and that—so it seems to me—will

[13] Cf. today: Sir John Eccles, *The Human Psyche* (Berlin and New York, 1980). Eccles postulates a "mind" that is independent from the activities of the brain.

[14] CW1, pars. 1ff. More details concerning Jung's early studies of a medium can be found in Stefanie Zumstein-Preiswerk, *C. G. Jungs Medium: Die Geschichte der Nelly Preiswerk* (Munich, 1975). Not all the information is quite accurate, however, because Mrs. Zumstein tries to turn Nelly Preiswerk into a heroine.

be a problem for future generations. Most modern theologians still try to discredit the irrational aspects of religion and use the most tortuous ratiocinations in order to "defend" religion, which they actually help to destroy.

The third lecture, Jung's inaugural address as chairman of the fraternity in 1897/98, needs no comment; it is understandable in itself. It shows mainly Jung's positive criticisms and postulates at that time. Much of it is as true today as it was then. Jung remained all his lifetime a "liberal" (in a nonpolitical sense) and voted seldom for the conservative Freisinnige Partei in Zurich, but rather for the Landesring der Unabhängigen (which since his time has changed in its policies).[15] For me, there is in the early formulations of this address a "heroic" undertone, an admiration or call for great political leaders, which the later Jung would not have maintained. The turning point in this respect came to him in December 1913, when he dreamed that he shot down the hero-figure of Siegfried.[16] Until then, I believe, he harbored the conviction that one could do something for mankind, or at least for European culture, that one could find new answers for our problem in *external* activities. The sacrifice of Siegfried put an end to this. From then on he let the primitive man who trusts the unconscious lead the way. All will to power, all temptation toward outer action was definitely given up, and Jung turned to his only task—the one he formulates himself at the end of this third lecture: namely that the Zofingia should "form human, not political animals, human beings who laugh and weep . . . who know that they are living among other human beings and that they must all put up with each other because they are all condemned to be human." How far are we still from this goal?

It was probably the Siegfried image in Jung's psyche that Freud sensed when he wanted to make him his crown prince and leader of the psychoanalytic movement, and that induced the later Jung to take steps to save the International General Medical Society of Psychotherapy, only leading him into trouble.[17] When he sacrificed "Siegfried" he was in accord with what the *I Ching* says, in hexagram 1, about the great man: "Wavering flight over the depths. No blame." And the commentary follows: "A place of transition has been reached, and free choice can enter in. A twofold possibility is presented to

[15] See V. W. Odajnik, *Jung and Politics* (New York, 1976).
[16] Memories, pp. 179ff./173ff.
[17] See Barbara Hannah, *Jung, His Life and Work* (New York, 1976), pp. 220ff.

the great man: he can soar to the heights and play an important part in the world, or he can withdraw into solitude and develop himself. He can go the way of the hero or that of the holy sage who seeks seclusion." Jung chose the second way and gave up his youthful idealistic postulates concerning outer reality.

The fourth lecture, "Thoughts on the Nature and Value of Speculative Inquiry" (Summer 1898), is a fascinating philosophical presentation. Some of its points perhaps call for comment today. After a discussion of the aims and meaning of science and the senselessness of external success, Jung sets two goals that seem to lead man to happiness: first, the fulfillment of Kant's *categorical imperative*, which would mean to follow one's innermost ethical conscience,[18] and secondly, what Jung then called (following Eduard von Hartmann) the "causal instinct," by which he means "the gratification of the causal instinct." The words "causal" and "causality" have today assumed a different meaning. What Jung there calls the "causal instinct" is in fact an individual urge to *understand* outer and inner reality, an innate passion, as he later called it in *Memories*, which he confesses to have been "the strongest element in my nature." He even calls it the possible reason for his birth on earth. "This insatiable drive toward understanding has, as it were, created a consciousness in order to know what is and what happens, and in order to piece together mythic conceptions from the slender hints of the unknowable."[19] In later days, Jung would have called this urge not a "causal instinct" but a drive towards the discovery of *meaning*. But that this idea was already present in the back of his mind is revealed by the fact that later in the lecture he calls this causal instinct the search for the truth and states that it inevitably leads to religion. For the present, he continues to describe this search for knowledge as "drawing inferences about the unknown, in accordance with the principle of sufficient reason," on the basis of real experience, and not drawing inferences about the inner world on the basis of the outer[20] or denying external reality by affirming only the inner world.[21] This is, in so many words, Jung's

[18] Cf. Jung's late paper, "A Psychological View of Conscience," CW 10, pars. 825ff.
[19] *Memories*, p. 322/297.
[20] As does materialistic science.
[21] As does, for instance, Hinduism.

scientific credo, to which he remained loyal throughout his life and upon which basis he called himself an *empirical* scientist.

In the next passage Jung explains why he uses the term (causal) instinct for this drive toward understanding—namely, because of its purposefulness, which is motivated "by a purposeful idea which is unknown to us." The causal instinct is "an ardent desire for truth" and a Faustian longing. Thus all philosophy develops finally into religion.

The ultimate causes toward which we advance our scientific questioning are always unknown or transcendental postulates, what Kant called the *Ding an sich*. But here Jung consciously describes Kant's *Ding an sich* in a completely new light. For him it belongs to "a world of the invisible and incomprehensible, a continuation of material nature into the incalculable, the immeasurable, and the inscrutable." Kant has shown that our mind is limited by certain inborn a priori categories, such as space, time, number, etc., and thus cannot recognize any *Ding an sich*, any absolute object. Jung accepted this view and thus for him the *Ding an sich* became the unknowable, whether an outer material or an inner psychic object. Kant's *Ding an sich* thus becomes, in his view, the same as that which Jung later called the background of the collective unconscious[22] or the *unus mundus* (in his late work *Mysterium Coniunctionis*). It is neither material nor inner psychic, but transcends our consciousness as something definitely unknowable. God in Himself and the background of the outer universe are such unknowable facts.

Later in the lecture it becomes clear that our unconscious hypothesis is also such an unknown factor, which, when it becomes conscious or known, ceases to be a *Ding an sich*. Here we can see a foreshadowing of Jung's later formulation of the archetype. It is an unconscious structure, unknowable in itself, which we can observe only in its manifestations as archetypal images, ideas, and emotions. An archetypal symbol, according to the later Jung, is dead and obsolete as soon as its content is known and can be intellectually formulated. Otherwise it contains a wealth of unknown aspects. The same is true for any scientific archetypal model or hypothesis—which Jung, in this lecture, calls principle.

Toward these principles or this principle (for they are a manifold

[22] He returns to this in a letter to A. Vetter, 8 April 1932. *Letters*, ed. G. Adler and A. Jaffé (Princeton and London, 1973), Vol. 1, pp. 90f.

One), science advances in a never-ending process. But this poses the question of whether there are one or two (or more) such principles. Jung first points out that Schopenhauer's basic principle, the Will, is an evolved interpretation of Kant's *Ding an sich*. It is unconscious because it created a world full of suffering, which Schopenhauer explains by the Will's *blindness* and Hartmann by saying that the *Ding an sich*, i.e., the transcendental ground of existence, is *unconscious*. They both come to this conclusion because they have feeling hearts for human suffering. This is, to my knowledge, the place where Jung first and with strong emotion formulated the *problem of opposites*. What in the observer is a conflict between monistic thinking and a feeling experience of the discord in life is in the general outer and inner world a play of opposites. Jung here stands up for a pessimistic dualistic view of the world, and he quotes Ecclesiasticus 33:15-16 and Jacob Boehme.

The latter part of the lecture, dealing with physics, is outdated in its details. What Jung seems to aim at is a double aspect of reality as being active, alive, creative versus passive, inert, and dead, a kind of opposition that strongly reminds one of the Yang-Yin philosophy of China (unknown to Jung then), with a one-sidedly positive aspect on the Yang principle. It is this one-sidedness of a purely masculine outlook on life that he later shot down in the dream-image of Siegfried. It was only after this that he could open himself up to the feminine principle and thus came, through his discovery of alchemy and his studies of it, to the concept of a *coniunctio oppositorum*, instead of holding to his pessimistic view of the world as a tragic and unending strife between the opposites. It was—as we can read here—the deep pity for the suffering of mankind that motivated his pessimistic view of life at that time and probably also motivated his becoming a doctor.

From these early torturing questions, which Jung poses in this lecture, we can also realize what a powerful experience the meeting with alchemy must have meant for Jung later, because alchemy is (as he himself has shown) a prescientific undercurrent that tries to reconcile and unite the cosmic and intrahuman opposites that the Christian outlook has torn apart. The blind Will of Schopenhauer and the unconsciousness of Hartmann's transcendental ground of existence thus lead a direct line to Jung's conviction that God, or the Background of Existence, is unconscious and needs man in order to become conscious (cf. *Answer to Job* and the chapter "Late Thoughts" in *Memories*).

The last lecture of this series (January 1899), leading into theological areas, is a direct continuation of what has been said before: it leads to religion. Just as Kant, after having stated the logical self-limitation of rational philosophical thinking, turned to the "starry sky above us and the ethical imperative within"—to a defense, that is, of religion—Jung was convinced that our deepest longing for consciousness is religious. We know now from his *Memories* that from earliest youth he had had deeply numinous religious experiences, but that he avoided talking about them because they seemed to frighten and estrange others. The contemporary trend, even in theology, was clearly against all mysterious, supernatural, and numinous aspects of religion. We know that Jung's own father's religious convictions were in his later life undermined by contemporary materialistic doubts, a fact that led to many fruitless discussions between father and son. Jung chose in his lecture to criticize the theologian Albrecht Ritschl in order to make his point. First he assembled a collection of Biblical sayings of Jesus, on which he based what he then wanted to convey, namely that Jesus was a god-man and as such a mysterious phenomenon that cannot be rationally explained. Such men "*are* their own idea, untrammeled and absolute among the minds of their age. . . . They have not evolved from any historial foundation, but know that in their inmost natures they are free of all contingency." It is noteworthy that Jung speaks here in the plural, that Christ for him was not the *only* god-man as Christian doctrine maintains. We know from his later writings that the Buddha was for him also such a god-man.

Then Jung branches out to show how, since the Renaissance, philosophy began to develop the idea of a "normal man" to which all epistomological results are *tacitly* referring and by which philosophers and theologians also began to "measure" the image of Christ. Later Kant regarded God as a "purely negative limiting concept"—all feeling has thus vanished from his concept of God and all possibility of a living experience of Him. And from there Jung goes into the details of Ritschl's "explanation" of Christ and Christianity. In themselves, Ritschl's views (which, by the way, influenced Karl Barth) are no longer of much interest, but the unfeeling ratiocinations of most theologians today are still in the same vein. When in a lecture some years ago I spoke of the resurrection

xxiii

of Christ, I was superciliously informed by a theologian that naturally the resurrection of Christ is not "true" as it is told in the Gospels, it is only a speech-image to describe Christ's continuing effectiveness in the world. Such ideas, Jung says, only satisfy the urge "to get a human slant" on Christ, a criticism he repeats *in extenso* in a letter to Upton Sinclair about his book *A Personal Jesus*, in 1952.[23] Other theologians nowadays follow Nietzsche's idea that "God is dead" or Freud's biological explanation of religion.

Viewed from this angle, Jung's criticism of Ritschl is still worth reading, for theology today is also poisoned with cryptomaterialistic reductive thinking. Any immediate experience of Christ or God, any *unio mystica*, is thus eliminated, and deadly boredom invades all our so-called religious life. But Jung goes on to say that it does not seem right on this account to throw away our whole Christian tradition. We "must accept the supramundane nature of Christ, no more and no less," and even more we must accept the "mystery," the world of metaphysical ideas to which Christ belongs and from which springs all religious life. But then—and here Jung touches in the end upon the great remaining problem—this would mean a return to the Middle Ages and a "concomitant disintegration of the existing order of nature." Because, Jung means, our civilizing achievement vis-à-vis nature would again be all undone. The lecture thus ends with an unanswered question, a question with which Jung struggled all his lifetime. In 1912 he came to the conclusion that he personally could *not* return to the medieval or original Christian myth[24] and set his foot on the path of finding his own myth by a form of meditation that he later called "active imagination." The world of images he discovered on this path seemed to him to be subjective and "strange" until, to his relief, he found their collective historical amplification: the world of alchemy. And there he also found how this world of alchemical religious symbols relates in a compensatory (but not opposite!) way to medieval Christianity, as he sets forth in his introduction to *Psychology and Alchemy*. This leads then in a direct line to what Jung sums up in the chapter "Late Thoughts"[25] as his real credo, where he expresses the idea that Christianity should not be discarded, but that its myth should be

[23] Letter of 3 November 1952. *Letters*, Vol. 2 (1975), pp. 87f. Cf. also the letter of 30 June 1956 to Elined Kotschnig, pp. 312ff.
[24] *Memories*, p. 171/166.
[25] *Memories*, pp. 327ff./302ff.

"dreamt on," evolved in order to answer the questions that medieval Christianity left unanswered: i.e., the integration of the feminine principle, as Nature or matter, into the too one-sidedly spiritualistic Christian symbolism and doctrine, and also an honest confrontation with the problem of evil, in the way he describes it in *Answer to Job*. Jung once said to me that he would like to rewrite all of his books again, except *Answer to Job*; that book could stay as it is, word for word.

MARIE-LOUISE VON FRANZ

I

THE BORDER ZONES
OF EXACT SCIENCE

(November 1896)

INTRODUCTION

1   My talk falls into three parts. First I will introduce myself. Second I will introduce you to me. Third comes the talk itself.

2   I would like the first part, my personal introduction, to bear the motto: "Woe unto him that sitteth in the seat of the mockers."

3   As many good citizens of Basel here present will gladly testify, my family, on both sides, have always been peculiarly given to offending well-meaning citizens because it is not our custom to mince words and, wearing an amiable smirk, to wheedle our honorable, highly estimable uncles, aunties, and cousins with flattering ways. It would also appear that I was born in an evil hour, for I always speak and behave just as my black heart prompts me to do. The resultant mental, verbal, and physical conduct is classified, in the inflexible columns of the great account book known as good breeding, under the headings "rudeness," "incivility," "impropriety," "insolence," "cheekiness," "unmannerliness"—all words that I invite you to look up in any pupil's register for the lower grades. I still suffer from this pathological trait and propose to turn it to good account right now, when fortune has decreed that I should bring in my sheaves—a time when it would be a great wrong to bind the mouth of the ox which treadeth out the corn.

4   (I account myself fortunate that the exalted, highly estimable and exceedingly wise "Committee for Public Welfare" has made it possible for me today to unearth a few pieces from the junkroom of my decrepit brain.)

5   It is customary to begin every lecture with a *captatio benevolentiae lectori sive auditori* (a petition for the indulgence of one's gracious reader, or rather, audience). For me it is even more essential than for others, to beg such indulgence. And yet so ignorant am I of the ways of the world that I really do not know how I am to cast my repellent person and repellent speech into such a mold as to merit indulgence. Regrettably it did not occur to me until yesterday that a Committee on Aesthetics has very sensitive ears which can tolerate neither a whoop of joy nor a raised voice, neither a vigorous

3

expression nor a boisterous phrase. I pray this exalted commission may pardon me and, if they please, graciously show me how to tone down my personality and my speech so that even sensitive freshmen can listen to my talk without suffering any damage to their aesthetic sensibilities.

6   I am well aware, inconsequential being that I am, that I as a person must be repugnant to a titular committee, as well as to every right-thinking citizen, and that what they would really like is to ship me off to hell, signed, sealed, and delivered. Thus I address to them the most lively entreaties that they lead this prodigal back onto the path of virtue—and not me alone, but also my friends, who are infamous and unscrupulous in the extreme. I beg that I— this black sheep which, alas, can do nought but bleat out what sheepish understanding inspires him to say—may nevertheless be accepted into the society of men, where people tell each other the truth only when they are intoxicated and where, when they are sober, they lie to each other with such disarming guilelessness that Their Honors the Devil and his dear grandmama really get a kick out of it all.

7   I welcome someone to instruct me how to acquire good breeding, and how to walk through the streets like a marionette with a fresh coat of paint on; how much a person has to lie before people will believe he is telling the truth; and how to emulate those virtues, possessed by a titular committee, which shine like beacons before us to show us the way.

8   If, during the talk which is shortly to begin, I should arouse universal displeasure, I ask that this be attributed to my naïveté, to the fact that I have not yet succeeded in plumbing the deeper mysteries of a semi-official tribunal whose members wear such a jovial and friendly mien.

9   I ask forgiveness if this introduction appears somewhat incongruous in the context of the title given my lecture, yet I could not very well have chosen a different approach, given the rule that one must pay people back in their own coin.

10   The purpose of this first part of my address was to introduce myself to you. The purpose of the second introduction will be to introduce you to me.[1]

---

[1] There is no indication in Jung's manuscript where the introductory part ends and the text proper begins.

THE BORDER ZONES OF EXACT SCIENCE

11   My intention, in venturing to dedicate my little talk to a theme unrelated to the most eminent aspect of our motto *Patria*, is to make a modest contribution toward the elucidation of certain questions that might have remained open in the intriguing talks of members of our local group during the last winter and summer semesters.[2] I speak of "certain questions that might have remained open" not because the papers just mentioned failed to do justice to their themes but, quite the contrary, because their exposition was so outstanding that they opened up a whole series of supremely interesting questions. For it is the hallmark of good papers or talks that they always suggest more of the scope of their subject-matter than they can actually treat.

12   Most of us heard both the aforementioned lectures, and no doubt all of us asked ourselves questions whose import transcends the confines of any single discipline and which must be of the most vital interest to every educated person. The problems involved are not a matter for specialists but for all human beings, and their objective or subjective solution is—or ought to be—the imperative concern of every thinking man.

13   As we all know, the principle of inertia is not confined to the field of physical phenomena but also represents a fundamental law of human thought. As such it is an even more powerful factor in the development of world history than stupidity.[3]

[2] *Marginal note*: (Cf. G. Pfisterer, "Die Herkunft der lebenden Wesen," *Centr. Bl.* August, 1896; and Stähelin, .)

Jung left the reference just so. Correctly: Georg Alfred Pfisterer, "Die Herkunft der organischen Wesen" [The origin of organic beings], *Centralblatt des Schweizerischen Zofingervereins* (Zurich), XXXVI:10 (July 1896), 609-631; and Karl Rudolf Staehelin, "Die verschiedenen Erklärungen des Lebens" [Divers interpretations of life], ibid., XXXVI:6 (April 1896), 387. Pfisterer (1875-1968), M.D., became a practicing physician with an interest in holistic medicine; Staehelin (1875-1943), M.D., became a professor of internal medicine, Basel University.

[3] Jung interpolated this paragraph and the five that follow, through the two quotations from Kant. He may have intended that the text proper follow thereafter.

14   This principle of *inertia*, innate to humankind, permits us to comprehend why nowadays, in the age of the hypercritical mind, we still see educated people in every walk of life—and not least among them physicians and natural scientists—who are not ashamed to proclaim their adherence to materialism, thus bearing witness to their own intellectual poverty. To be sure, one cannot blame these people too much, for they are only aping a well-known model, that is, parroting what Papa DuBois-Reymond is saying in Berlin.[4] After all, we cannot demand that everyone should think for himself. Given this fact, the ultimate solution might be a "revolution from above," but any revolution of this kind will be a long time coming, and it will take the labor of several decades before the inert masses are set in motion. Although I know it is a waste of energy for me to combat materialism, nevertheless I hope to help draw a clearer portrait of this absurd colossus with feet of clay.

15   To this end, in the present study I attempt to supply a critical description of the theories and hypotheses of the exact sciences, insofar as these play a decisive or fundamental role in contemporary attitudes. I will discuss only those theorems absolutely essential to my exegesis, and of these only the most important and the best known.

16   The principal purpose of this critical exercise is to point up certain contradictions. If it remained faithful to this character, its result would be negative, taking the form of an insoluble dilemma. But as no reader would be satisfied by this, I have undertaken to draw the obvious conclusions from my results, in order to reveal the necessary metaphysical presuppositions of any physical process. This will make it possible to counteract the purely demoralizing effect of the critique, and we will arrive at a positive result which might serve as a solid point of departure for further critical excursuses in the realm of metaphysics.

4 Emil Heinrich DuBois-Reymond (1818-1896), a native of Berlin and professor of physiology at Berlin University, founded the modern science of electrophysiology and was the first to study electrical activity in nerve and muscle fibers. He collaborated with German physiologist Hermann von Helmholtz, and the two of them, with Carl Ludwig, influenced biological thought in Europe through their attempt to reduce physiology to applied physics and chemistry. This approach had a deep impact on the psychological theories of Freud and helped to strip from physiology all vitalist theories which regarded matter as arising from a "life force." Later in these lectures Jung alludes to this "mechanist-vitalist controversy."

17   I could, in my view, choose no better *captatio benevolentiae* than two quotations from Kant, with which I introduce my essay to the public:

18   "For every substance, even a simply material element, must possess an internal activity as the cause of its external operation."[5]

19   And: "Whatever in the world contains a principle of life appears to be immaterial in nature."[6]

20   As we all know,[7] there are people—I am speaking only of so-called "educated" people—who knock about the world packing a whopping bundle of erudition, but who, down to the day they reach "the cold, cold grave," do nothing but label the contents of their bundle as conscientiously and meticulously as they can, and whenever a favorable opportunity presents itself, open up their little store of goods and bask in the reverent awe of the uninitiate. But in the process they neatly discard anything and everything that might in the slightest way disrupt the sublime order of their little curio shop. Disagreeable troublemakers who want something other than second-hand bric-a-brac are gotten rid of, by means that are quite aboveboard, at the first convenient opportunity. This tactic guarantees the reign of universal peace in the realm of science, and friction between individual scholars over issues involving their specialties only sets this in sharper relief. The scholarly world as a whole is like an ocean whose mirror surface remains serene and flawless. Everyone is happy, and people raise each other's spirits by pointing out that everything has been explained and divided into beautiful, orderly, functional compartments. To be sure, no one person knows everything, that is, no individual run-of-the-mill scholar knows everything, but he has access to all the help he needs, in the form of people known as "authorities on the subject," i.e., people who, as everyone is aware, know more than ordinary scholars and who, in all seriousness, assure us that everything is going smoothly and functioning just as it should. However, as a rule there is no need to summon these temporary emergency assistants, as

---

5 Immanuel Kant, *Träume eines Geistersehers, erläutert durch Träume der Metaphysik* (Leipzig, 1899), Part I, p. 15. (Tr. E. F. Goerwitz: *Dreams of a Spirit-Seer, Illustrated by Dreams of Metaphysics*, London and New York, 1900.)

6 Ibid., p. 14.

7 In the holograph, this paragraph and those that follow until the asterisk are stricken out by a light line of the pen.

for their day-to-day needs people can rest serene in the mere knowledge that these "authorities" exist. In fact it is said that a great many—who knows, perhaps most—just swim along with the tide without even needing to rely on this reassuring thought. They are the luckiest of all, educated people like children tasting honey, who can nibble at the sweetness of scientific knowledge with impunity. They are free to enjoy, more or less innocently, the golden light of day. For them there are no questions, no riddles, nothing exalted and nothing profound, no bright and no dark. Their thoughts and feelings, their philosophy and their religion, culminate in a single thought: a certain individual exists, his name is such and such, he lives there and—vegetates.

21   Have I gone too far, I wonder? I think not. But a simple method exists by which to determine the accuracy of my portrayal: let us simply ask ourselves the question, what are the subjects that interest people most, and to what field do these subjects belong?

22   To answer this question I shall allow myself to pick only a few blossoms from a garland and offer them to you like a little nosegay.

23   If I were to select only the most extreme examples of those subjects that are of interest to educated people, I would first be compelled to find an audience that has forgotten how to blush. For nowadays it is by no means rare to see an educated man, even a scientist, weltering in the vilest slime.[8] But there is no reason to discuss this, for such conduct is also quite unpopular even with so-called educated people. Instead let us choose another showpiece from the junkroom of erudite absurdity. Something really impressive: Mammon. Anyone who is not interested in money in one form or another, is deemed to have played his cards all wrong and missed out on the real purpose of his life. It might be worthwhile, for once, to estimate approximately how many people belong to that great confraternity who strike up a Te Deum when the interest rate rises 1 percent. Naturally I would also include in this group all persons who study for venial purposes or who have set their sights on "marrying well."

24   Are we perhaps being overly conservative if we estimate that 90 percent of all educated people belong to the great "Salvation Army"? I think we can be content with this figure as a start.

[8] *Deleted sentence*: The discriminating intellect of man is operating on a level that would disgust a pig.

25   I will take the liberty of stating my humble opinion: I consider it disgraceful for an educated man to accept the idea of the preeminent power of money. It is even more disgraceful if he tips his hat and shows his reverence to a sack of gold. But it is most disgraceful of all if he uses—or rather abuses—his knowledge and skills to gain bliss from the one thing that can give it, the personal possession of Mammon.

26   Ought I perhaps to cite a few shining examples to substantiate my claims? Ought I to tell you about all those who engage in scholarly pursuits merely in order to fill up as quickly as possible the moneybag that they have invested with the sacred aura of scientific knowledge? Shall I tell you of those savants whom others regard as having attained the pinnacle in human perfection, but who sell their science and their knowledge for thirty pieces of silver?

27   I will not speak of these people. I will hold my tongue, for I have resolved not to become personal.

28   I will just remind you of that nice saying: "For cash you can buy them anywhere: scholars and—whores!"

29   Another showpiece, no less impressive, is the desire to be regarded as successful, to have a so-called "career," and the slaves of this drive are known as "careerists." They work, they strive, they race through life at breakneck speed—not for the sake of their fellow men and not even for their own sakes, but rather for the sake of a fiction, a hallucination. With superhuman energy, they squander their lives, violate truth and justice, and frenetically destroy their own happiness and that of others, in order to snatch at a glittering phantom born of their own overheated imaginations: glory in the eyes of others.

30   There have always been "careerists"; that we must concede. But in the past they represented only a drop in the bucket, whereas today they can be measured by the bushel. It is an important sign of the times that such people should exist, people who pride themselves on being skeptics, who are radical in a way that makes a simple man cringe, and who venerate, as the highest goal of their lives, a mad farce, an insubstantial ideal which radiates contempt for all rational attitudes. They laugh at the simple faith of the unsophisticated, and meanwhile kneel in the dust before the idolized abomination created by their own diseased imagination.

31   Ominous indeed is this comet which is lighting for our dying century its path into the grave.

9

32   There, we have just plucked three venomous blossoms for our little nosegay. Now let us turn our attention to a few other, more innocent "flowers of the grass" which the little educated lambkins like to nibble on.

33   I suggest that we drop in on a group of educated people at suppertime and listen to their interesting conversation.

34   The educated housewife or her spouse, the master of the house, plans to entertain this evening's guests with talk about the theater, a concert, and all sorts of aesthetic and artistic affairs, with a bit of popular science thrown in for good measure. And of course a scrap or two of politics should also liven up the party.

35   So everyone rattles away in the most amiable fashion about the aforementioned topics. They express moderate praise or mild censure concerning a current theatrical presentation, as well as about yesterday's concert. They get a little more stirred up about the exhibit at the art gallery, but are careful not to voice any extreme opinions that might conceivably be contradicted by one of the others. With an indulgent smile they recall the rather caustic review in the papers, and laugh just enough but not too much about a painting that has been damned by public opinion, with their hands in their pockets at the same time to show that they have their own independent views on the matter. Then they all have a swig or two of wine and move on to politics. Naturally they cannot neglect to mention the horrible things going on in Armenia. In well-chosen, polite phrases they express their view that it is a little strange of the Turkish sultan to torment the poor Armenians so. One guest tells another about the latest news bulletins, which he has just read in the papers; his partner politely plays along, saying that he really has not heard anything about the matter yet and that he is extremely interested in the fate of the good Armenians. Next someone brings up the subject of X-rays, and then it's time to go home. Everyone was absolutely enraptured by the evening, and they all swear to high heaven that they found the conversation exceedingly lively and witty.

36   If we add these blossoms to our nosegay, we have a picture of the whole of educated society and its spheres of interest.

37   So, when we turned to people whom we expected to exhibit some depth, behold, they were all drowning in the waters of shallowness. Is it not a sad thing to see people with academic training, who at

matriculation swore a noble oath to dedicate their lives to science and truth, ending up in this swamp?

38   As for us, will we too end by succumbing to these same treacherous shallows of banality? Will we, like these others, one day merit the reproach that we buried the precious talent[9] entrusted to us? Do we not have a sacred duty to guard the youthful germ-seed of awakening knowledge from the death-dealing frost of indifference?

39   We must ask questions, we must search for truth, we must struggle to attain knowledge, we cannot do otherwise. Those numbskulls who are too lazy to open their eyes and see, and who play dead whenever they have the good fortune to come face to face with a problem, are pretty pathetic specimens. Unfortunately educated people know how to behave like mealworms just like everyone else.

40   But what is the reason for the unfathomable apathy displayed by educated people today? Actually there are a number of causes. First, there are the hordes of inane books which are devoured with such ecstasy and keep minds busy with other matters. Second, there is the universal *modus vivendi* of our age, in which one studies in order to earn a good living later on, and concentrates on one's own specialty. Third, there is the dogma that science actually explains some things. And fourth, there is the wholesale indifference, where they don't give a damn about what or how or why they are studying.

41   There has never been an antidote to indifference, and as the saying goes, "the gods themselves cannot defeat stupidity." We have no choice but to rise above it.

*

42   When a nonscientist asks us about the results of the exact sciences, as a rule we talk—if the field is physics—about the laws of gravitation, and about wave and ether theory;[10] in the field of chemistry about atomic and molecular theory; in zoology and botany about equivocal generation,[11] heredity and natural selection; in physiol-

9 "Talent" as in the Gospel parable, Matthew 25:14-28.
10 In late 19th-century physics, ether (German *Aether*) was a hypothetical medium for transmitting waves of light and heat, filling all unoccupied space. Einstein's introduction of the special theory of relativity in 1905 eliminated the need for the hypothesis.
11 Equivocal generation involves the theory that organic life can spring from inorganic sources.

ogy about mechanism and vitalism. If a scientist is honest, he concludes his remarks with a shrug of the shoulders. But as a rule scientists do not do this, for it looks better to pose as an oracle spouting dogmas. It's more impressive.

43 But if we ask ourselves, in all earnestness, whether things really are as we scientists have represented them or whether they simply look that way, we see quite a different picture. One system, one theory after the other starts to waver. Many remain with blurred contours, whereas others collapse altogether. For example, let's take a look at the theory of ether, based on the theory of light, heat, and electricity. Our question is: Is there really such a thing as an ether, do we have proofs of its existence? There are no conclusive proofs, nobody has ever perceived the ether, in any way, shape, or form, by using his normal five senses. Thus the most obvious conclusion is: There is no such thing as an ether. Yet its existence is a necessary postulate of reason. How are we to conceive and imagine motion, that is, expressions of force, divorced from a body? How can vibrations occur in the absence of a body to do the vibrating? How can light be conducted through an absolute vacuum? How can an electrical spark travel from place to place without a conductor? And yet all these phenomena do take place. Light travels immeasurable distances through the great vacuum between the stars to get here, and lightning streaks out of the clouds to the earth. Thus there must be a body, a conductor, to transmit these manifestations of energy. But this body is not perceptible to our senses, is not subjective or objective in any way. It is completely immaterial and yet has material properties perceptible to our senses. Thus there is a collision between reality and reason. Doesn't this collision represent a grave violation of the completely materialistic and skeptical attitude of modern science? Dare we call this an "explanation," this thing that runs counter to all common sense?

44 Scientists do not like to talk about the ether, for it is awkward to have to deal with properties and forces that do not appear to be linked to a body. If we expand the implications of this dilemma, we see that it is an absolute requirement of reason that unless we assume the existence of an ether, we must conclude that the existence of light is also illusory. But if an ether does exist, then reason in turn requires that light has the characteristics of an imperceptible body, a body that is in the fullest sense of the word metaphysical, that is, immaterial.

12

45   But where does this simple mental exercise lead us? The most
elementary train of reasoning has suddenly transported us from
the realm of the most concrete phenomena, into a realm where we
must confront the most despised word in the field of applied science, namely "metaphysical." Is it really the spirit of exact science
that has directed us onto this path? It must be, for the result we
have arrived at is the obvious conclusion we must draw from the
facts.

46   Properties without a body to possess them may find themselves
in a truly tragicomical situation. So does a body that possesses an
impossible property. The body in question is matter itself. As we
all know, it is an innate property of all bodies to exert a mutual
attraction. This phenomenon is known as universal gravitation. An
attempt to account for the attraction leads us into the most ominous
circular arguments. For the concluding argument is always the
same: Bodies attract each other—because it is a property of bodies
to do so. How are we to picture this attraction? The fact that it
takes place is beyond question; but how, by what avenue? *How* can
this bodily property manifest itself in the body? A force is exerted
that is transmitted from one body to another. Thus it must follow
a certain route in order to arrive at the other body. But how is it
transmitted? As we have already seen, a force without a conductor
is an absurdity. Thus to get from *A* to *B*, the force must find a
carrier or conductor. Does the ether obligingly perform this function? In this case the force would move from one atom of the ether
to another. But this would simply mean that for the time being the
property of the body is transmitted to the atoms of the ether. But
if the atoms possessed this property, they would attract each other,
and a concentric conglomerate of ether would form around *A* and
B, and then the transmission of force from *A* to *B* would come to
a halt. Or are we to describe the ether as inert or neutral with
respect to the force of gravitation? This would be a completely
transcendent explanation—i.e., it would go far beyond our conceptual powers. For how can we imagine a property transmitted
by a body that is wholly neutral in relation to this property? The
very definition is self-contradictory. It is absolutely impossible for
a conductor—supposing that it is to function as a conductor in the
first place—to assume the property in question for the time being,
without assuming its characteristic manifestations, i.e., in effect
without assuming the property at all. For the conductor would have

13

to be constructed in such a way that it assumes and transmits a property without taking over the property as such. But this notion is so baffling that we have finally returned to a metaphysical hypothesis. For it would be too flimsy to explain one hypothesis in terms of another.[12]

47   And again, what is the relation between the problem of mutual attraction and the law of the conservation of energy? Probably no law of nature has ever received such repeated and universal confirmation. We are virtually *flooded* with proofs which stream toward us from the realms of both organic and inorganic nature. Without this law all the theories and experiments of the physical sciences would be impossible. The law of the conservation of energy tells us that a certain quantity of energy remains constant under all circumstances, i.e., that for every force there exists an equivalent force whose decrease is proportional to the increase of the first force. If we look at any energy source, for example, an electrical plant that supplies such-and-such a quantity of energy per day, where does the energy come from and what is its equivalent? Its equivalent is found in the kinetic energy of the waterfall whose power we tap with turbine engines. But where is the energy equivalent of the waterfall? It resides in the potential derived from its position—i.e., in the fact that the water falls from a higher to a lower place. The water derives the potential energy of its position from the heat of the sun, which has heated it to the evaporation point and thus elevated it to its present location.

48   It will not be necessary to elaborate further on this example. The meaning of the law must, I believe, be clear to everyone.

49   Now let us apply this law to our problems of universal gravitation. What is the energy equivalent of gravitational force? For it must have an energy equivalent if we are to continue to regard the law of the conservation of energy as universally valid.

50   Gravitational attraction never ceases, for every body continually exerts gravitational force, applying unvarying pressure to its place of rest. Thus gravitational force by no means ceases when the body is at rest. The attraction does not become latent in a state of rest, but is manifested as a constant degree of gravitational force. But where does the body get this energy? We must assume that it gets

---

[12] *Deleted*: Moreover, we have reached the border of something that simply leaves science behind.

it from inside itself. In this case it possesses, as a part of its substance, a force equivalent to gravitational force. Thus according to the rules, certain changes must take place in the body that cause the force to develop. These changes must necessarily be material if they are to result in the production of a force that can be materially demonstrated. But material changes are subjectively or objectively perceptible by our senses, and thus the energy equivalent of gravitational attraction must be verifiable. However, in reality we cannot verify any force equivalent to gravitational force. No changes take place either inside or outside the body, which remains unaltered year in, year out, always maintaining a constant level of gravitational force. We must rest content with this circular argument: Matter exerts gravitational force because it is a property of matter to exert gravitational force. Once again we confront a collision between reason and reality. Reason demands an equivalent force, reality has none.

51   It would be a gross error to cite this finding as an argument invalidating the law of the conservation of energy. For if we look at the situation more closely, we see that we do not need to apply this law to universal gravitation, insofar as universal gravitation represents its point of departure. For the law merely expresses the constancy of a certain quantity of energy, and we are looking at that quantity right now. Universal gravitation represents that same specific quantity of energy whose constancy and modifications are defined by the law. The energy equivalent, which we might desire to define in terms of a higher spatial concept, is not available to us; it lies in the absolute.

52   Now let us turn to the atomic and molecular theory that is the basis of the system of modern chemistry. I trust that my gracious audience will spare me the labor of employing many words and arguments to elucidate the contradiction that exists, in the concrete, between reality and the postulate underlying the system. I will merely draw a quick sketch of the collision between the logical consequences of the system and the actual state of affairs. This problem, too, is of subsidiary importance, as what we see here is not a discord between reality and the claim of reason, but merely the collision between reality and a system that is not in absolute accord with reason.

53   We imagine matter to be composed of atoms. The atom is, by definition, a body that cannot be subdivided further, that is, a body

without extension and thus a mathematical point. Here we see a patent contradiction: Matter has extension, and thus it can never be composed of parts without extension.

54   A far more important problem, and one of more general interest, is the province of the biological sciences, zoology, botany, and physiology; and we should include psychology as well. I am referring to the question of the origin of life.

55   It seems best if, in our critical examination of this question, we strike out on the same path which the problem itself took in the course of its evolution. Twenty or thirty years ago, the debate over the original creation threw the entire scientific world into an uproar. A heated battle raged, and rages still. The flames were not extinguished with the final refutation of Dr. Bastian.[13] The embers are still glowing beneath the ashes, and are flaring up again these days in the struggle between mechanism and vitalism. The question has not changed. It is still the same old question, only now it is cast in far more general and dangerous terms. What is involved here is not an insoluble contradiction between reality and the claim of reason, but rather the most violent collision between two claims, both of which are consistent with reason. At stake is the "to be or not to be" of the modern, materialist-skeptical view of nature.

56   If we trace back to its beginnings the course of the evolution of organic life, we arrive at the first cell, rocked by the warm waves of the primordial sea and dimly sensing an unknown world to come. The cell is there, and with the cell there is life. This is a brutal, incontrovertible fact. But what existed before the cell, when the hot vapors had not yet condensed around the edges of the glowing, molten ball of the earth? What was there *before*? Has organic life been there from the beginning, as matter is said to have always existed? But then how could it have survived amid the flaming chaos, the white-hot vapors of iron and platinum? Or is life perhaps a function of matter? If so, the original creation was guaranteed from the outset. Matter would have had a free hand to produce whatever forms struck its fancy. But it is a fact, verified by a hundred thousand cases, that organic beings never develop out of inorganic matter, but only through contact with life. If ever a law was absolute, then it is this, that *omne vivum ex vivo*. Practical reason (empiricism)

[13] Henry Charlton Bastian (1837-1914), British neurologist, was an advocate of the theory of spontaneous generation. See his *The Beginnings of Life* (London, 1872).

requires that never, under any circumstances, shall a capricious, random occurrence intervene in that drama of nature which unfolds according to eternal laws. Yet on the other hand, pure reason (logic) requires that the existence of an organic being presupposes contact with life. Which claim should we consider justified? On the one hand, no one has ever observed a sudden arbitrary disruption of the lawful course of phenomena; on the other hand, it is equally correct that no one has yet verified a breach in the continuity of all phenomena. We see that in both cases the grounds for the claim are the same rational ones. Which claim outweighs the other? The claim of logic demands something that empiricism, on the same grounds, must categorically deny.

57   Let us take a critical look at these claims. What is the basis of the claim of empiricism? It is based on the fact that no analogous case has been observed in the past. What is the basis of the claim of logic? The fact that many thousands of such cases have been observed in the past. The "empirical" proof is negative, the "logical" positive. The scale tips in favor of the claim of logic. The results: The creation of the first cell must have come about through contact with preexistent life. For reasons already enumerated, it is impossible that this preexistent life was linked to matter, and thus it must have existed independently of matter, i.e., immaterially. Isn't this strange? The critical examination of rational scientific claims leads us into an immaterial or metaphysical realm.

58   It will not be necessary to engage in a critical examination of vitalism, for in the foregoing excursus we have already discussed the principle involved, citing the example of equivocal generation. My audience is quite capable of drawing the conclusions with regard to vitalism.

59   Now let us turn back to our nonscientist friend, the one to whom, a short while ago, we recited the results of science in such an authoritative tone. What does he have to say about all this? Won't he consider it strange and presumptuous on our part if we dare to speak about scientific "results"? Indeed, it would almost seem that there are no such things as results. Science has not actually explained anything. And if science thinks it has explained something, it has done so with a hypothesis. Whenever we look for the true "reason why," we reach the great nothingness, a realm of the vaguest hypotheses. Our wisp of intelligence simply ceases to function at the point where the true explanation begins. We have no

choice but to confirm the operation of causality in the realm of concrete phenomena, but can we explain it? Never. In view of all this, isn't it rather foolish for people to get so terribly worked up over Darwin's theory of the origin of species, when this theory expresses nothing substantial? The "Why?" lingers in the background; it is and remains inexplicable.

60 Our friend the nonscientist will go away shaking his head, thinking his own thoughts about the famous "enlightenment" shed by science.

61 But what do we have to say about the matter? Can we wrest nothing at all from universal nothingness? Or is there after all a possibility that what seems to us impossible may turn out to be possible? Does that Ariadne's thread which has led us this far really end abruptly in the darkness, or does it perhaps continue, leading us out of the night and into the light?

62 We imagine that we have arrived at the end. But in fact we are only at the beginning. We think that the gate is locked, when we have the key. Science supplies us the raw material; why don't we go on building? We have the basic premises; why do we resist drawing the conclusion?

63 We have seen that the ether, with its transcendental properties, constitutes an essential means of explaining certain physical phenomena, just as a preexistent vital principle is necessary to explain the world of organic phenomena. Let us enter both into our scientific computation under the designation X. We have positive knowledge of a limited number of properties of both these phenomena. Our natural inclination is to regard these properties as the only properties that they truly possess. But are we right? The most recent events in the world of science teach us that we have no choice but to adopt a passive attitude and to simply wait and see what more nature will choose to reveal to us. Doesn't Roentgen's discovery clearly demonstrate that the ether possesses other properties in addition to those that were already known to us?[14] An even more striking example of the changes in human knowledge is the triumphal entry of hypnotism into the domain of German science. After a century of struggle, public attention has finally been drawn to this new aspect of the vital principle. Such phenom-

[14] W. C. Roentgen (1845-1923) discovered X-rays in 1895, at Würzburg University, one year before the composition of this Zofingia lecture.

ena surely ought to prevent us from jumping to hasty conclusions, and from claiming that now all aspects of life have been fully explored. The position of contemporary skeptical materialist opinion constitutes, simply, intellectual death. This attitude actually prohibits us from overstepping narrow boundaries. It condemns us to go on gathering data for storehouses that have long been filled to the brim. We improve our microscopes, and every day all they do is to reveal to us new and greater complexities. We improve our telescopes, and all they do is to show us new worlds and systems. The riddle remains, and the only change is that it grows ever more complex. We behold the infinity of the world in the microcosm, we behold it in the macrocosm. Where does it all end?

64   Why do we long to exhaust the ocean of infinity when we do not yet even know the banks of the pond where our materialist-minded savants are croaking away like frogs?

65   We just stated that we have admitted two metaphysical principles into the realm of material nature. The physical phenomena have been studied and threshed out down to the last detail. Metaphysical phenomena are virtually a closed book. Surely it would be valuable to inquire into properties other than those with which we have long been familiar. Our critique of the two problems more or less compels us to acknowledge their existence. An immaterial phenomenon that manifests itself only materially: Is that not an irrational claim? Is it not in fact sheer nonsense?

66   Can we imagine a body without properties? I think not. At least I would like to meet a man who was capable of doing that. Thus it is impossible for any such thing to exist. Can we conceive of a material body without material properties? This is impossible; the very idea is a contradiction in terms. But can we conceive of an immaterial body without immaterial properties? Yes indeed, for nowadays virtually the entire scientific world is doing just that. But we do not want to go along with the crowd. What we want is to allow the immaterial to retain its immaterial properties.

19

II

SOME THOUGHTS ON PSYCHOLOGY

(May 1897)

GENERAL INTRODUCTION

67 Some of you may recall the talk I gave during the last year's winter semester. What surprised people most about that talk was the introduction, and I repeatedly heard it said that one of the hardest things on earth is to achieve a smooth transition from the introduction to the exposition. In order to smooth the way for my talk today, I would like to introduce it with these divine words from the psychology of Immanuel Kant:

68 "Morality is always paramount. It is the holy and inviolable thing which we must protect, and it is also the reason and purpose of all our speculations and inquiries. All metaphysical speculations are directed to this end. God and the other world are the sole goal of all our philosophical investigations, and if the concepts of God and the other world had nothing to do with morality, they would be worthless."

69 Ever since my last paper narrowly escaped sudden death in the wastebasket, I, ἄσμενος ἐκ θανάτοιο,[1] have been wanting to have a chance to walk with you along the Stygian banks to the realm of the shades.

70 Despite the fact that, by using a little imagination, we can realize that certain things are conceivable and posit certain others as necessary, nevertheless most of you will feel a scholarly shudder of dread if we actually leave behind us the broad road of everyday experience, with its solid foundations, to descend into the nocturnal abysms of nature.

71 No doubt people will call it an act of mad adventurism to abandon the safe path laid out for us by esteemed science and accredited philosophy, to make our own independent raids into the realm of the unfathomable, chase the shadows of the night, and knock on doors which DuBois-Reymond had locked forever with his little key that says "Ignorabimus." People will accuse us of fancifulness

[1] "Glad from death," a phrase occurring frequently in the *Odyssey* whenever the band of adventurers leave behind them some peril which has claimed the lives of one or more of their number.

72 and superstition. With a superior smile they will reach out to grasp the iron laws of nature and strike the rebels dead with them. Those who will do this are the same people who fill every Sunday of their lives chockful of edifying words, deeds, and thoughts, but on weekdays parade around with a sign that says "We will never know." They will claim that ours is a fruitless and a hopeless enterprise, a self-tormenting brooding on the absurd. In the apt phrase of Schwegler[2] in his history of philosophy, these people are the devotees of a "man-in-the-street philosophy" who, as such, "make a completely erroneous use of the category of causality."

73 Doubtless the most vehement protests will be voiced by those who, out of sheer indifference—or because, in plain language, they don't give a damn—have become intellectual teetotallers and who, by the mere fact of their existence, pronounce the harshest anathema over even the most tentative effort to stimulate interest in certain questions. Despite all this, and despite the danger of arousing the keenest displeasure, I have chosen to speak on this theme before all others. Left to my own devices, I might well tremble for the fate of my cause, but I have allies. They belong not to the ranks of the known exiles and heretics—among them revered and brilliant figures such as Crookes, Wilhelm Weber, and above all Zöllner[3]—but rather are men of such reputation that one need have no qualms about citing their authority. I have selected three such men, whose critical powers and keenness of judgment are beyond all question. As my first authority I cite David Strauss[4] in his classical evaluation

---

[2] Albert Schwegler (1819-1857), author of *Geschichte der Philosophie im Umriss* (tr., *A History of Philosophy in Epitome*, New York, 1856).

[3] Sir William Crookes (1832-1919), English physicist and chemist who discovered cathode rays and isolated thallium. Wilhelm Weber (1804-1891), German physician who studied electromagnetic induction. Johann Karl Friedrich Zöllner (1834-1882), astrophysicist and devotee of spiritualism.

[4] David Friedrich Strauss (1808-1874), Protestant theologian and author of an influential *Life of Jesus*, included reviews of the books of the spiritualist physician Justinus Kerner in the collection *Charakteristiken und Kritiken: Eine Sammlung zerstreuter Aufsätze aus den Gebieten der Theologie, Anthropologie und Aesthetik* (Leipzig, 1839). Part II of Strauss's essay collection includes a review of Kerner's *Beobachtungen aus dem Gebiete kakodämonisch-magnetischer Erscheinungen* (1834; Essay VI in Strauss), and Strauss's Essay XI is a "Kritik der verschiedenen Ansichten über die Geistererscheinungen," both essays being discussions of Kerner's observations of a woman who saw and conversed with benign and malign spirits and produced knocking and other phenomena of the "poltergeist" type in the presence of witnesses.

of Justinus Kerner and the Seeress of Prevorst[5] in *Charakteristiken und Kritiken.*[6]

74   He writes concerning the Seeress: "Her face, suffering but with noble and tender features, suffused with a celestial radiance; her speech the purest German; her talk gentle, slow, solemn, musical almost like a recitative. Its content, rapturous emotions which drifted across her soul, now like soft and fluffy clouds, now like dark stormclouds, and then dissolved. . . . [Her] conversation with or about blessed or accursed spirits [was] conducted with such truth that we could have no doubt that we were truly in the presence of a prophetess who partook of communion with a higher world. . . .

75   "We in no way share the opinion of those who attack the truth of Kerner's account, in part accusing the sick woman of dissimulation, in part imputing to the physician a consistent failure to perceive what was really going on—a supposition which not only eyewitnesses like the author, but also all unbiassed readers of Kerner's account, can recognize as groundless."

76   As my second ally I cite Arthur Schopenhauer, who states in his *Parerga und Paralipomena*: "It is not my vocation to combat the skepticism of ignorance whose cavilling deportment brings it into disrepute every day."[7] "Nowadays anyone who doubts the fact of animal magnetism and the clairvoyance it confers, must not be called skeptical but ignorant."[8] Schopenhauer wrote this almost fifty years ago.

77   The third ally I will cite is our great master Immanuel Kant, the sage and prophet of Königsberg who has, not unjustly, been called the last philosopher.

78   One hundred years ago, Kant in his lectures on metaphysics, in Part Two of the rational psychology, stated: "We can conceive of spirits only as problematic entities, i.e., we can cite no a priori cause *to reject their existence*." "Something can be admitted, on a problematical basis, provided that it is quite clear that it is *possible*. We cannot demonstrate apodictically that such spirits should exist, but neither can anyone disprove it."

79   One hundred and thirty-four years ago, in the *Dreams of a Spirit-*

---

[5] See n. 4. Jung subsequently cited Kerner's work on the Seeress of Prevorst, notably in his M.D. dissertation: see CW 1, pars. 49-148 *passim*.

[6] See above, n. 4.

[7] Schopenhauer, *Parerga und Paralipomena* (Berlin, 1862), p. 243.

[8] Ibid.

Seer, Kant recorded the following confession, which is of great significance in relation to his views as a whole: "I confess that I am strongly inclined to assert the existence of immaterial natures in the world, and to class my own soul among these beings."[9]

80   Elsewhere Kant states: "All these immaterial natures, I say, regardless of whether or not they exercise their influence in the corporeal world; all rational beings which happen to exist in an animal state, whether here on earth or on other heavenly bodies, regardless of whether they animate the raw stuff of matter now, will do so in the future, or have done so in the past, would, by these terms, exist in a communion suitable to their nature, not determined by those conditions which limit the relations of corporeal entities, and in which the distances separating places and times, that in the visible world create a vast gulf abolishing all communion, simply disappear. Accordingly it would be necessary to regard the human soul as already, in this present life, linked with two worlds of which, it being joined in personal union with a body, it clearly perceives only the material; whereas on the other hand, as a member of the spirit world, it receives the pure influences of immaterial natures and distributes these influences in turn, so that as soon as its union with the body has ended, nothing remains but the communion in which it continually dwells with spiritual natures, and which must reveal itself to consciousness as an object of clear contemplation."[10]

81   Finally, in a third passage, casting his prophetic gaze far beyond his own age, Kant states: "Accordingly it has in effect been demonstrated, or could easily be demonstrated if we took a broad view—or better yet, it will be demonstrated in the future, I know not where or when—that even in this life the human soul dwells in an indissoluble communion with all the immaterial natures of the spirit world, alternately affecting these natures and receiving from them impressions of which, in its human nature, it is not conscious *as long as all goes well.*"[11]

82   It would probably be my best course to end my talk at this point, for after such illustrious minds as these have had their say, it seems almost blasphemous to tack on the paltry appendix of my own

9 Kant, *Träume eines Geistersehers, erläutert durch Träume der Metaphysik* (Leipzig, 1899), Part I, p. 14.
10 Ibid., p. 20.
11 Ibid., p. 21.

thoughts—thoughts which, to use an unattractive simile, are like witless, broken-winded plant lice creeping up a magnificent tree with wide-spreading branches.

RATIONAL PSYCHOLOGY

INTRODUCTION

83   "Well, that's all just as nice as pie," says the educated philistine, "but I don't believe in things unless I see them with my own eyes. And what you call metaphysics has been out of date for a long time, nobody takes it seriously any more, and if any metaphysical notions are still around today, it's only in the form of an obsession that haunts people who are not yet at ease with themselves. Everything in the life of a rational man unfolds on a completely physical and natural plane."

84   Yes indeed, until we reach DuBois-Reymond's stockade everything is perfectly clear and comprehensible, and everything which "the Lord God made" ought to be grateful that finally a public benefactor has built a stockade at this dangerous frontier. One feels so safe and snug inside its four walls, and so let's not have any miracles, for that would disturb the peace.

85   To be sure, there is nothing very wondrous in the life of the hidebound educated philistine. He is born, he grows and develops himself, for a higher level of functioning demands differentiated organs. Then he marries, in accordance with his character and aims. He begets children through the union of the sperm cell with the egg cell. His children are blessed with the attributes of their parents, in accordance with Hertwig's theory of heredity.[12] Then little by little he grows old, even though this fact no longer fits so well into the system. And then, what happens then? Then something happens that no longer fits into the system at all, that is completely incomprehensible, the clarification of a lie, the emendation of an error:[13] he dies—! Why? For what purpose? His doctor cold-blood-

[12] The 1892 edition of Oscar Hertwig's *The Cell and the Tissues* (tr., London, 1895) was the nineteenth century's most trenchant synthesis of biological phenomena under the aspect of the universality of protoplasm.
[13] *Originally*: the terrible clarification of a shameful lie, the ghastly emendation of an error.

edly records: death by violence, disease, old age. In short, the game is over. The corpse is lying there cold and stiff, and shortly thereafter protein decomposition sets in. It is an incredible fact, and if it had happened only once, to only one person, no one in the world would believe it could happen at all. But the same thing happens to us all, and it is irrevocable. The average life lasts barely thirty years. But why does death occur? Why should an organism constructed with infinite care and efficiency, whose innermost purpose it is to live, come to an end, wither and decay? Why is the purposeful drive to live cut off with such contempt? Death impresses us as a brutal infringement on our most exalted and sacred right, our right to exist. A sudden blow, and all our plans, all our hopes, all our joyous creativity lie shattered. And how treacherously this infringement occurs! It is impossible to discover anything that is actually *done* to the organism or taken away from it. If we weigh the dead body, it weighs exactly as much as it did when it was alive. The entire organism is there, complete, ready to live, and yet it is dead and we know of no art to make it live again.

RATIONAL PSYCHOLOGY

86   It is a strange Something that is removed from the body, a Something that contained the will to live, a force that in life maintained an accord between the organism and its environment. It appears to be an elementary force, a vital principle. In earlier times physiologists used to call it the life force, thereby making a correct application of the "category of causality." Kant says: "It appears that an intellectual being is intimately present with the matter to which it is joined, and that it does not act upon those forces by which the elements relate to each other but rather upon the inner principle of their state."[14]

87   Modern physiology has no name for this "intellectual being" that acts on the "inner principle," for once again it naïvely confuses the effect with the cause—as I dare to assert despite the dressing-down I received in my semester report.

88   The physiologist Burdach,[15] one of the much-despised vitalists, states in his work *Physiologie als Erfahrungswissenschaft*: "Materialism

[14] Kant, *Träume eines Geistersehers*, p. 15.
[15] Karl Friedrich Burdach (1776-1847), comparative anatomist and physiologist. The work cited was on physiology as empirical science.

presupposes that life which it sets out to explain. For the organization and the blend of components from which it derives the life processes, are themselves the product of a life process." The old vitalists made many mistakes, but never have they sacrificed the basic requirements of logic to the interests of their system.

89   The vital principle, which as long as life lasts confers on the body its power of resistance, is the enduring factor in the phenomenal realm. As we know, all the molecules in the body are renewed approximately every seven years. Thus the substance of the body is continually changing. If the life-organizing, life-shaping force resided in matter, nothing would be more natural than a continual transformation of the appearance of the body. But this does not actually occur, for the external traits of a man remain the same. All down to the smallest details are preserved. All the images in his memory remain constant, and his intellectual faculties maintain approximately the same level. In short, despite the change in his substance the individual remains the same. Thus it appears that the *principium vitae* constitutes, so to speak, the scaffolding on which matter is built up.

90   Burdach states: "The matter of our bodies continually changes, whereas our life remains the same, remains one. Corporeal life is embraced in the continual, simultaneous destruction and formation of organic matter. Thus life is something higher, which dominates matter. . . ."

91   But if we turn our attention to more recent physiology, what a strange spectacle we see. Physiologists are struggling to explain life in terms of natural laws, when all the time it is clear that life exists *despite* these laws. They try desperately to force life into the system of natural laws, when life contradicts every law of nature. Spontaneous motion violates the law of gravitation; the very existence of the body violates the laws governing oxygen affinity and the biological laws governing bacterial activity. In Volume I of *The*

92   *World as Will and Idea* Schopenhauer aptly remarks: "It is becoming increasingly apparent that a chemical phenomenon can never be explained in terms of a mechanical phenomenon, nor the *organic* in terms of the chemical or electrical. Those who today are nevertheless striking out once more on this old false trail, will soon creep back, quiet and crestfallen, like all their predecessors."[16]

[16] *Die Welt als Wille und Vorstellung* in Schopenhauer's *Sämmtliche Werke*, Vol. I (3rd edn., Leipzig, 1877), § 7, p. 35.

93   If we subject the phenomenon of organic life to the principle of sufficient reason—that is, if we apply the "category of causality" correctly—then it is as necessary for us to postulate the existence of a vital principle as it is to postulate the ether in the field of optics. This postulate does not violate the first principle of the scientific method, namely that the principles used to explain a phenomenon must be kept to the barest minimum. In the present case we are compelled to admit a new principle, for no previously existing principle furnishes an adequate explanation.

94   What is true of the individual is true of all: Darwin's theory of natural selection cannot adequately explain evolution, and indeed, with regard to the evolution of new species it becomes a negligible factor. In the field of phylogeny, more than in any other, it is necessary to postulate the existence of a vital principle.

95   The vital principle is more or less equivalent to the "life force" of the ancient physiologists. It governs all bodily functions, including those of the brain, and hence also governs consciousness to the degree that consciousness is determined by the functions of the cerebral cortex. Thus we ought not to seek for the principle of life within the consciousness, and most particularly not in the consciousness of the self, as Kant did.

96   The vital principle extends far beyond our consciousness in that it also maintains the vegetative functions of the body which, as we know, are not under our conscious control. Our consciousness is dependent on the functions of the brain, but these are in turn dependent on the vital principle, and accordingly the vital principle represents a substance, whereas consciousness represents a contingent phenomenon. Or as Schopenhauer says: "Consciousness is the object of a transcendental idea." Thus we see that animal and vegetative functions are embraced in a common root, the actual subject. Let us boldly assign to this transcendental subject the name of "soul." What do we mean by "soul"? *The soul is an intelligence independent of space and time.*

97   1. *The soul must be intelligent.* The criterion of intelligence is the purposefulness of its acts. Undeniably our bodies impress us as highly purposeful, and thus we postulate the intelligence of the soul. If the law of causality did not possess an a priori status, this postulate would be proven.

98   2. *The soul must be independent of space and time.* The concepts of space and time are categories of the understanding and for this reason are not compelling with regard to the *Ding an sich*. The soul

eludes all sense perception and thus cannot constitute any form of material force. Only forces in a material form constitute objects of perception. But within the categories of space and time, judgment is based on sense perceptions. Accordingly only forces in a material form can serve as objects of judgment, i.e., only forces in a material form move within the boundaries of space and time. For example, let us consider the concept of velocity, which is equivalent to the space-time quotient. Or think of any of the basic mechanical laws of physics.

99   The soul does not represent a force in a material form, and thus there can be no judgment concerning it. But everything that cannot be judged subsists outside the concepts of space and time. Accordingly the soul is independent of space and time. Thus sufficient reason exists for us to postulate the immortality of the soul.

EMPIRICAL PSYCHOLOGY

INTRODUCTION

100   Up to this point we have been treading on the consecrated ground of Kantian philosophy. But who will accompany us further if we choose to burst open the gates that bar our entrance into the "realm of darkness"?

101   Is it not maddening when Kant himself says: "Experience cannot possibly teach us that there exist beings which possess only an inner sense"? (*The Psychology*)[17]

102   Or in another passage: "We can say nothing more about these spirits, such as what a spirit can achieve separated from the body. They do not constitute objects perceptible to the external senses, and thus they do not exist in space. We can say nothing beyond this; if we did we would only be spinning idle fancies." (*The Psychology*)

103   Or in another passage: "I dare say that this observation (of mine) . . . represents all that philosophical insight can reveal about beings of this kind, and that although in the future we may continue to have all sorts of notions about them, we can never know more than we do now."[18]

104   Kant could not help but speak as he did, and from his own standpoint he was absolutely right. More than one hundred years have passed since he said these things. In this time a lot has happened to confirm his words, and to amplify their meaning in unlooked-for ways. Kant's epistemology endures unaltered, but his dogmatic teachings have undergone changes as must occur with every dogmatic system. No fresh genius has appeared to supplant Kant's ideas. What have supplanted his ideas are facts whose validity is beyond all doubt.[19] Today, as Wallace[20] accurately notes, we can

[17] *Vorlesungen über Psychologie* (1889).
[18] Kant, *Träume eines Geistersehers*, p. 42.
[19] *Deleted*: facts which only a fool could deny.
[20] Alfred Russel Wallace (1823-1913), English naturalist and a founder of zoological geography.

simply smile and pass by those persons whom laziness or rabid skepticism cause to deny certain extrasensory data.

105   It was impossible for Kant to have known the facts in question, and that is why he could not have spoken otherwise than he did. Baron DePrel[21] says—quite rightly—that if Kant were alive today, he would undoubtedly be a spiritualist. Kant spared neither time nor effort to get in touch with Swedenborg.[22] Insofar as it lay in his power, he tested the validity of Swedenborg's claims and gave them a thorough and unbiased reading. What a contrast lies between this greatest of all sages ever born on German soil, and his puerile epigones, who do themselves the honor of citing Kant and yet do all they can to suppress and ridicule something that can only confirm Kant's profound ideas!

106   And people do show what fools they are when they use Kant's ideas to attack the spiritualists, when Kant himself said:

107   "It will be demonstrated in the future, I know not where or when—that even in this life the human soul dwells in an indissoluble communion with all the immaterial natures of the spirit world, alternately affecting these natures and receiving impressions from them. . . ."![23]

108   Kant said this more than one hundred years ago, when he could have had no inkling of the facts relating to modern spiritualism.[24] Almost sixty years ago Schopenhauer raised his voice against "the skepticism of ignorance."[25] Even he, the pessimist par excellence, was an optimist to the extent that he could describe skepticism as daily coming "into increasing disrepute."[26] In the mid-1870s William Crookes, the English chemist and physicist who had been challenged by the entire body of the English press to investigate spiritualism, submitted to the Royal Society his classical report on the subject, containing the most comprehensive confirmation of the validity of spiritualistic phenomena. Around the same time Russel

---

[21] Baron Karl Ludwig August Friedrich Maximilien Alfred DuPrel (1839-1899), celebrated spiritualist, who published as Carl DuPrel.

[22] See Kant's letter to Charlotte von Knobloch in *Träume eines Geistersehers*, pp. 69-75 (quoted in CW 18, pars. 707-9).

[23] *Träume eines Geistersehers*, p. 21.

[24] Much of what Jung reports here on spiritualism reappeared in his lecture "On Spiritualistic Phenomena," originally in *Basler Nachrichten*, 12-17 Nov. 1904 (CW 18, pars. 697ff.).

[25] Schopenhauer, *Parerga und Paralipomena*, p. 243.

[26] Ibid.

Wallace, famed for his role in the history of Darwinism, likewise wrote a variety of texts in which he fought for justice and truth. In 1877 the noble Zöllner[27] published his scientific tracts in Germany, and fought for the spiritualist cause in a series of seven volumes. But his was "a voice crying in the wilderness." Mortally wounded in his struggle against the Judaization of science and society, this high-minded man died in 1882, broken in body and spirit. To be sure, his friends, the renowned physicist Wilhelm Weber,[28] the philosopher Fechner,[29] the mathematician Schubner, and Ulrici, continued to promote Zöllner's cause, while the stubborn Wundt,[30] the slippery Carl Ludwig,[31] and the spiteful DuBois-Reymond defamed this cause throughout a Germany in moral decline. All in vain—the Berlin Jew came out on top. The little group of the faithful melted away. The only educated champion of spiritualism in Germany is Baron Carl DuPrel, who, however, is being doggedly ignored. In Russia there are two men with scientific training who defend the cause of spiritualism: the aged privy councilor Alexander Aksakov[32] in St. Petersburg and Wagner,[33] professor of zoology at the University of St. Petersburg. In 1892 two Italians, the astronomer Schiaparelli,[34] noted for his study of Mars and director of the Osservatorio di Brera, and Lombroso,[35] the renowned anthropologist and psychiatrist, declared their belief in spiritualism. The latter did so with the classical confession: "I pride myself on being the slave of facts." An index to the more liberated thinking of the English was the founding of the *Dialektische Gesell-*

[27] Johann Zöllner's *Wissenschaftliche Abhandlungen* were published in Leipzig in 1878-79.
[28] See above, n. 3.
[29] Gustav Theodor Fechner (1801-1887), German philosopher and a founder of psychophysics, the study of the relations between mental and physical processes.
[30] Wilhelm Wundt (1832-1920), German philosopher and psychologist who viewed metaphysics, ethics, and the intellectual from a psychological perspective.
[31] Carl Ludwig (1816-1895), German physiologist whose work helped to defeat the vitalist school.
[32] Alexander Aksakov (1833-1903), a student of medicine and psychic phenomena, author of *Animismus und Spiritismus* (1890), and opponent of Eduard von Hartmann's views on spiritualism.
[33] Probably Julius Wagner (1857-1940), Austrian physician.
[34] Giovanni Virginio Schiaparelli (1835-1900), Italian astronomer who discovered the markings on Mars thought to be "canals."
[35] Cesare Lombroso (1836-1907), Italian physician who believed that criminals were sick rather than evil.

schaft, composed exclusively of professional scholars, which I believe was an offshoot of the British Association.

109   In Germany—and Switzerland—there seems to be no sign that men like Kant, Schopenhauer or Zöllner have ever lived. Gone and forgotten! People will not even listen to Eduard von Hartmann, a philosopher who is now very much a la mode, and his theory of the unconscious, much less to DuPrel, who deserves closer study. What we hear from the rostrums of science is the thousandfold echo of materialism. This loathsome, stinking plant is being grown in all the scientific institutions in the land and well-nourished with the dung of the career men. A professor drowned in mechanistic psychology and nerve-and-muscle physics[36] is sowing the poisonous seed that fecundates confused minds—minds that then bear splendid fruit, incomparable rubbish, some thirty-, some sixty-, some one hundredfold. Gradually the mud is seeping down from the heights of the university. The natural consequence is the moral instability of the upper echelons of society and the total brutalization of the working man. The results: anarchists, anti-socialist laws, and so on. Naturally the clergy make a great to-do about the steady progress the devil of unbelief is making in the hearts of men, but this does not prevent them from mounting the pulpit and inveighing against the sin of spiritualism and stuffing people full of all sorts of old wives' tales about the spiritualists. Thus without realizing it the clergy are encouraging the general moral debacle, and the police, the guardians of the law, are contributing to the same end by prohibiting spiritualistic fraud. Every rational man, who believes that everything in life is purely "natural"—for example, the schoolmaster—rages and campaigns against this medieval nonsense which is threatening to extinguish the lamp of his enlightenment. The worthy educated philistine who believes in nothing he cannot see, blindly places his faith in every anti-spiritualist canard, every wretched lie the journalists tell him, and voluptuously wallows in the quagmire of literature on the subject published by the "progressive" press. Radiating bliss, he reads Ludwig Büchner's *Kraft und Stoff*,[37] a work to which the remark of the

[36] The reference is to work of the physiologist DuBois-Reymond.
[37] *Kraft und Stoff: Empirisch-naturphilosophische Studien* (Leipzig, 1868). (Tr. J. F. Collingwood, *Force and Matter: Empirico-Philosophical Studies*, London, 1864.)

old Göttingen professor Lichtenberg[38] aptly applies: "If a head bumps into a book and the result is a hollow sound, is that always the fault of the head?"

110   If anyone ever writes the natural history of the educated philistine, the chapter on *laziness* would have to take up half the book. Kant says at one point: "Laziness and cowardice are the reasons why, long after nature has emancipated them from the governance of others, such a large proportion of people are quite content never to grow up all their lives."

111   It is unnecessary for me to comment further on this quotation, for it expresses my view to a tee. Thus there is no better course than to add my endorsement.

EMPIRICAL PSYCHOLOGY

112   In the second part of my talk, which deals with empirical psychology, I will supply documentary evidence which should satisfy those many people who were not entirely happy with the theoretical reflections in the first part. On the other hand, this same factual evidence will put off many who were, in principle, satisfied with the theoretical exposition in Part One.

113   In research we are completely dependent on the empirical method, just as we are in our practical everyday lives. Intuition does not have the power to convince the critical mind, any more than theoretical considerations can show us how to deal with practical situations. And yet, strangely enough, any number of people who are in perfect agreement with the findings of rational psychology, refuse, for various reasons, to admit that psychology possesses an empirical side. In plain language, in Basel there are hundreds, perhaps thousands of people with adamant faith in the miracles of the Old and New Testaments, but who would not for anything in the world admit that identical or similar events are still taking place today. Again, there are people who, on the theoretical plane, accept the existence of the soul and its possession of any number of possible attributes, but who refuse to admit that anyone can have practical experience of such things. As for those people who don't care about anything and who only exist to mark the dark shadings in the picture of life, we need not speak of them at all.

[38] Georg Christoph Lichtenberg (1742-1799), physicist, professor at the University of Göttingen.

114   The primary concern of empirical psychology is to supply factual documentation supporting the theories of rational psychology. The first principle of rational psychology, concerning the existence of the soul, does not require factual documentation. If we make correct use of the "category of causality," we must necessarily affirm the existence of the soul. Naturally people who do not employ the category of causality, or rather who feel no need for it, are not competent to voice an opinion in this matter. The number of facts supporting the existence of the soul is legion. If the soul did not exist, it would be impossible for these facts to exist. But because there is no such thing as an impossible fact, the soul must exist.

115   One of the principal tasks of empirical psychology is to provide detailed authentication of the definition of the soul laid down by rational psychology. We have already noted that the soul is an intelligence independent of space and time.

116   1. *The soul is intelligent.* The principal proof in support of this principle is the purposeful activity of the soul, its power of organization. Its organizational activity is manifested in the phenomenon of *materialization*. I cannot assume that everyone in my audience knows the meaning of the term materialization, and so I must beg those who do to pardon me if I interrupt my remarks for a moment to explain.

117   The soul is imperceptible to the senses because it exists outside space. It would have to assume a spatial, i.e., a material form in order to become perceptible to the senses. Every representation of the soul that is perceptible to the senses is a materialization. The most wondrous and incredible materialization which has ever occurred is man himself. But most people are incapable of marveling at their own existence and thus cannot properly appreciate the notion of man as a materialization of soul, and thus we must look about for other phenomena whose spontaneous and instantaneous manifestation compels us to deduce an intelligent being as their *spiritus rector*. The phenomena we seek are the wondrous materializations observed by Crookes, Zöllner, Wilhelm Weber, Fechner, Wagner, Wallace, and many others. In 1873 Crookes and Varley, a member of the Royal Society, succeeded, with the aid of the medium Florence Cook, in producing a manifestation in their London laboratory and in repeatedly photographing it, under electric light, together with the medium. After countless failures Professor Wagner, with the assistance of Frau von Pribitkov, succeeded in

photographing a hand above the medium's head in a room at the University of St. Petersburg. As far as I know, Zöllner, Wilhelm Weber, and Fechner, who from 1877-1879 conducted joint experiments with the medium Dr. Stack, did not take any photographs, but did obtain a series of handprints and footprints on soot-blackened paper laid between two pieces of slate.

118 In 1875, for the first time, paraffin molds were taken of hands that spontaneously materialized in space. This feat was achieved by William Denton, a geology professor at Wellesley College in Massachusetts († 1883), while he was on a geological expedition in New Guinea. Since that time these experiments have been repeated, with great success, in England and on the continent. I myself have in my possession photographs of such phenomena, and anyone who would like to see them may do so at any time. It would be easy to go on and on citing pieces of evidence that substantiate the idea of the intelligent organizational activity of the soul. But given the limited scope of my talk, the examples I have already cited must suffice. If anyone is interested in pursuing these topics, I recommend that he study Zöllner's *Wissenschaftliche Abhandlungen* and Alexander Aksakov's *Animismus und Spiritismus*, as well as the treatises of Crookes and Wallace in Mutze's Spiritualism Library in Leipzig.

119 We have yet to document the second element in our definition of the soul: *The soul is independent of space and time.*

120 Everything that lies beyond our conceptual categories, i.e., beyond space and time, is transcendental. Everything transcendental, that is, everything nonspatial and nontemporal, will always be incomprehensible to us, and in this sense the claim "Ignorabimus" is entirely justified. Our confrontation with the transcendental is not confined to the psychical realm of sensory experience. Instead, people have been able to experience it in their everyday lives ever since 1687, the year which saw the publication of Isaac Newton's *Philosophiae naturalis principia mathematica*. Universal gravitation, representing as it does a long-range effect (*actio in distans*), is the direct manifestation of a transcendental principle, as I explained last semester in my critique of the law of gravity.

121 Gravitation is purely transcendental. Its successful emancipation from space and time is achieved, above all, by virtue of the fact that it does not conform to the law of the conservation of energy as an elementary force; secondly, because by virtue of gravitation,

corpus ibi agere non potest, ubi non est (a body does not exert effects in a place where the body itself is not); and thirdly, because it does not require time for its deployment, for it is absolutely constant. This is the characteristic of the long-range effect, the *actio in distans*.

122   The soul, as the metaphysical presupposition of the phenomenon of organic life, likewise transcends space and time, and for this reason its emancipation from sensory manifestation must be expressed in the fact that the soul appears as the basic force of *actiones in distans*. Thus to substantiate the second clause of our definition of the soul, we must present evidence substantiating the *actio in distans*.

123   The best course, to present our evidence in the most lucid and intelligible form, is to divide the discussion into two parts treating 1) long-range effects in *space*, and 2) long-range effects in *time*.

124   The topic of long-range effects in space will be divided into *telekinetic* and *telepathic* phenomena.

125   *Hypnotism* should be classed among the telekinetic phenomena. There is no need for me, in this context, to go into further detail concerning hypnotic phenomena, as a first-rate talk has already been devoted to this subject. I will merely recapitulate briefly what has already been said. Hypnotism involves the establishment of a so-called rapport, an intimate bond, between the agent and the percipient. We know that the means for establishing such a rapport include causing the percipient to gaze at a fixed point, and in general, stimuli of a monotonous nature. If the agent or percipient possesses a special aptitude, phenomena can be intensified. The agent can move three, four, or five steps away from the percipient. In one case the famous mesmerist Hansen succeeded in withdrawing eighty steps. An even higher level is achieved if the agent remains in a separate room. With a particularly sensitive percipient, the agent can remain twenty, thirty, or more kilometers away and still achieve a rapport. When a high degree of psychic excitation is present—for example, in cases involving dying persons—distance in no way limits the phenomenon. I assume that there is no need for me to furnish documentary evidence, as doubtless everyone has experienced, or heard of, such cases in his own family.

126   Intimately related to these phenomena is that of the *Doppelgänger* or double. On occasion a dying person who, from a distance, communicates to a friend the knowledge of his impending death, can

intensify hypnotic perception to the point of inducing a hallucination, and indeed may often create an actual, objective manifestation capable of producing material effects.

127   During the appearance of an authentic *Doppelgänger* (eidolon), the agent is generally in a deep, self-induced somnambulistic trance. However, this is not always the case. There are cogent reasons to believe that the degree of awareness characterizing the *Doppelgänger* is inversely proportional to that of the living agent.

128   Also to be classed among telekinetic phenomena are all those material effects produced, for example, by dying people in order to communicate to faraway relatives or friends the knowledge of their death.

129   *Telepathic phenomena* include clairvoyance, which occurs in space. In certain cases the sensitivity of the percipient to telekinetic effects might also be designated as telepathy. However, this sensitivity represents telepathy only to the extent that it outweighs the active psychic power of the agent. In this case we see genuine clairvoyance on the part of the percipient. All the obstacles presented by space have vanished. It is as if the soul were wandering about free of all fetters, having escaped the body's onerous husk. A classic example of clairvoyance, which has been authenticated by reliable historical sources, is cited by Kant in his letter about Swedenborg, to Fräulein Charlotte von Knobloch.[39] In this letter Kant describes how Swedenborg, while he was in Gothenburg, had a clairvoyant vision of the great fire which took place in Stockholm in 1756, and how hour after hour he reported to the horrified public the progress of the fire. All this happened on a Saturday evening, and it was not until the evening of the following Monday that a messenger arrived in Gothenburg on horseback bringing the news from Stockholm. A number of skeptics, in order to come up with a natural explanation of this extraordinary event, actually went so far as to accuse Swedenborg of having set the fire himself!

130   We can content ourselves with this one example of clairvoyance, for it would be virtually a waste of time to cite additional cases. Anyone who has ever taken a look at the relevant literature can easily discover any number of cases substantiating this phenomenon. Recommended reading for anyone interested in this subject

[39] See above, n. 22.

is DuPrel's *Fernsehen und Fernwirken*, Volume II of his *Entdeckung der Seele*.[40]

131   The theory of long-range effects in time[41] is among the most obscure and complex topics in the realm of occult phenomena. Under this heading we classify premonitions, prophecies, second sight, and clairvoyance in the strict sense. I have not gone into any explanation of the phenomena previously discussed because any such explanation would lie far beyond the scope of my talk. For the same reason I will refrain from any attempt to explain long-range effects in time, despite the fact that the problem is vitally interesting and virtually begs for commentary. However, I cannot resist the urge to at least hint at the direction that an explanation might take. To this purpose I cite Schopenhauer's statement in the *Parerga und Paralipomena*:

132   "Consequent upon Kant's doctrine of the ideality of space and time we understand that the *Ding an sich*, in other words the only reality in all phenomena, being free from these two forms of the intellect (intellectual categories), knows nothing of the distinction between near and far, between present, past and future. Accordingly the divisions based on these modes of viewing the world show themselves not to be absolute, but instead, in terms of the mode of cognition we speak of, which is substantially altered by the modification of the organ [of cognition], no longer present any insuperable barriers."[42]

133   There seems no need for any extensive treatment of examples. I will merely recall the famous tale of the Cossack who predicted the downfall of Poland many years beforehand, and the case of Cazotte, who in the year 1788, according to the account of a witness, François de la Harpe of the Academy, prophesied the terrors of the French Revolution, telling each person present the manner of his death in every detail.[43] I would also remind you of a case close

[40] *Die Entdeckung der Seele durch die Geheimwissenschaften* (2 vols., Leipzig, 1894-1895). See above, n. 21.

[41] In the margin here, Jung jotted a rubric, *Actio in distans in d. Zeit*, then crossed out *Actio* and wrote *Passio*, though elsewhere he retained *Actio* in the phrase.

[42] Schopenhauer, *Parerga und Paralipomena*, p. 280.

[43] *Marginal note*: J. Scherr, *Blücher* I, p. 259.

    The reference is to *Blücher, seine Zeit und sein Leben* (3 vols., 1862-1863), by the historian and literary scholar Johannes Scherr. The work is in Jung's library. For Blücher, see below, Lecture III, n. 5.

to home: I learned from a thoroughly reliable source, namely the attending physician, that a female patient suffering from hysteria prophesied, in obscure words, the disaster of Münchenstein, several months before it occurred. When the disaster ensued, the woman was in upper Switzerland, whence she clairvoyantly perceived the catastrophe at the same moment that it took place. An inquiry dispatched immediately by telegram confirmed the accuracy of this clairvoyant vision.

134 Prophetic dreams, which represent a lower level of conscious clairvoyance, also belong in this category. One special form is the "second sight" of the Scots, a gift that actually afflicts vast numbers of people on the solitary isles of northern Scotland. The Old Testament prophets may also be described as clairvoyants, despite the fact that in recent times strenuous efforts have been made to reduce to a minimum all the miraculous elements of the Bible, and to divest its mystical protagonists of their characteristic nimbus. This has been done with apparent disregard for the fact that it turns the prophets into caricatures, hack journalists who mystify the public with their prophecies *after* the prophesied events have already taken place. Quite apart from the insipidity of such an interpretation, it would never have occurred to any Jew to follow the behests of such straw men.

CONCLUSION

135   We have now reached a definite result: We have succeeded in providing empirical evidence substantiating our definition of the soul. To be sure, many people may be amazed by this novel and singular procedure, and many may find it difficult to breathe because of all the dust kicked up by outraged conservatives.[44] For the foolish misgivings and critical shrugs, the foot-dragging refusal to reach any decision, the citing of a priori principles to obscure and ignore problems, the narrow-minded pedantry and the parochial skepticism, border on the ridiculous. Like Schopenhauer I can say: "It is not my vocation to combat the skepticism of ignorance." I can only laugh at those dandies of skepticism and of fashionable doubt. Soon the unceremonious Homeric laughter of posterity will mingle with the sound of the bells ringing out to proclaim the disgrace of a Germany overcome by materialism. Despite semester reports and the Central Committee, I will now say what I believe to be the truth.

136   One day people will laugh and weep at the same time over the disgraceful way in which highly praised German scholars have gone astray. They will build monuments to Schopenhauer, who linked that materialism with bestiality through the conjunction "and." But they will curse Carl Vogt,[45] Ludwig Büchner, Moleschott,[46] DuBois-Reymond, and many others, for having stuffed a passel of materialistic rubbish into the gaping mouths of those guttersnipes, the educated proletariat.

137   They will fetch out Schopenhauer's *Parerga* and bombard the materialists with the same words with which Schopenhauer lam-

[44] *Deleted*: It is high time that we look and see what lies under the dust: gold or dung.

[45] Carl Vogt (1817-1895), German naturalist who advocated the biological theory that living organisms have changed in the course of the various geological epochs—i.e., an evolutionist.

[46] Jacob Moleschott (1822-1893), Dutch physiologist, philosopher, and advocate of materialism.

basted Hegel—only worse. Hegel was accused of having paralyzed young people's minds, castrated their intellect, dislocated their heads, and disordered their brains. The same accusations will be leveled against materialism, which will be held responsible for the fact that everything and everyone is going to the dogs; that it officially declared the reign of mindlessness and funneled into our brains the foolish twaddle about the eternity and sublimity of the inflexible laws of nature; that it poisoned morality and induced the moral instability of the educated classes.

138   How are we to counteract this lamentable debacle? In the first place we must institute a "revolution from above" by *forcing* morality on science and its exponents through certain transcendental truths, for after all, scientists have not hesitated to impose their skepticism and moral rootlessness on the world. In institutions that offer training in physiology, the moral judgment of students is deliberately impaired by their involvement in disgraceful, barbarous experiments, by a cruel torture of animals which is a mockery of all human decency. Above all, in such institutions as these, I say, we must teach that no truth obtained by unethical means has the moral right to exist. In these public institutions, designed as havens for the study of life, people ought to engage in experimental research into psychic phenomena, and these places should be staffed with far-seeing, freethinking men, not homespun philosophers[47] with "dislocated heads." I have said that we must combat crass sensualism with the weapon of certain transcendental truths. But whence are we to derive these truths? From religion? The theologians, the administrators of religion, have been shouting themselves hoarse for years trying to fight the demon of disbelief. Ever since Hegelian philosophy and current religious orthodoxy ceased to be a going concern, people have been coming up with all sorts of novel notions, not a few of which we owe to a certain Ritschl.[48] But the sermons we are hearing give us no clue as to who really has something special to tell us, for among the products of this century is an execrable jargon of the pulpit, the "language of Canaan," which is used to cover up anything that might possibly offend anyone. If we listen to certain sermons without any preconceived ideas, we will soon find ourselves all agog with notions about grace and plans of sal-

[47] *Originally*: intellectually impotent philistines.
[48] See Lecture V, below, for a discussion of Albrecht Ritschl.

vation. The clergy speak this way to the educated and workers alike. The latter are in the cure of the Christian Socialists,[49] who expend great enthusiasm but with little success. The aim is to wake up religion, put life back into the Christian faith, but it's all in vain! Nowadays the masses no longer want to believe. (They picked up this little trick from the upper crust.) They want to *know*, like the scholars who are also immoral unbelievers. What use are words in a case like this? What use is all the idealism in the world? *Deeds* are needed to wake up religion, miracles are needed, and men endowed with miraculous powers. Prophets, men sent by God! Never has a religion sprung from a dry theoretician or a gushy idealist. Religions are created by men who have demonstrated with deeds the reality of mystery and of the "extrasensory realm." The dry postulates of reason and mere religious feelings cannot redress the ravages of our age; the only thing that can do that are facts that directly establish the validity of something beyond the senses.

139   Of course we must never fall prey to the illusion that the majority of men will ever be capable of appreciating the value of a fact. For deep inside human beings is a sediment of passivity, a tenacious, primordial slime out of which an act of first creation daily generates an infernal mental indolence.

140   Whenever God succeeds in creating a Faust, the calculating devil gets busy and releases one hundred thousand hidebound intellectual philistines from Hell so that they can grab hold of this Faust's coattails as he is trying to "rise up out of this sea of absurdity,"[50] and hold him down with the sticky glue of their boundless indolence. The educated philistine is characterized by laziness, cowardice, parochialism, and the total lack of any "metaphysical hungers." On Sundays he populates the churches en masse, and until dinnertime rolls around he busies himself with the most edifying words, deeds, and reflections. In the afternoon he is sweet-tempered, well-behaved, and good. In the evening, as a rule, he pretends to be a connoisseur of music or goes strolling outdoors to commune with nature, seeking inner peace in the open book of Creation. Generally he is in a very uplifted frame of mind, and has a keen sense of

49 The Christian Socialist movement in Germany, led by the Court preacher Adolf Stoecker from the late 1870s onward, tried to appeal to the German working class with a program combining paternalistic welfare measures and loyalty to church and state. (D. S.)

50 *Faust I*, "Outside the City Gate," line 1065.

duty. But beyond this there is nothing to the man, he trails off into a great wasteland. There is not a trace in him of any vivacity, any energy, any enthusiasm. He hates, fears, and disparages everything he is not used to. The faithful allies of the educated philistine are that great flock of flimsy butterflies and moths whose traits can be summed up in a single word: *inconsequential!* Intellectual ephemera flitting from one little swamp to the next, and blown about by every breeze.

141 It seems that I have made myself clear. But I know that dregs are dregs and remain at the bottom of the cup. But I may be forgiven for my optimism if I hope that my appeal today has made some impression on a few minds that are still flexible and uncorrupted. If this hope proves vain, I can nevertheless console myself with the knowledge that I have done my duty:

> He who knows the truth and does not speak it
> Is a poor wretch indeed.[51]

142 The new empirical psychology furnishes us with data ideally designed to expand our knowledge of organic life and to deepen our views of the world. They enable us to glimpse nature's abyss, to gaze into an intelligible world where the eyes seek in vain for any shore or any limit. Nowhere do we feel as keenly as here that we are living at the boundary between two worlds. Our body formed from matter, our soul gazing toward the heights, are joined into a single living organism. We see our lives coming in contact with a higher order of being. The laws governing our mental universe grow pale before that light, emanating from the metaphysical order, which it is granted us to dimly divine. Man lives at the boundary between two worlds. He steps forth from the darkness of metaphysical being, shoots like a blazing meteor through the phenomenal world, and then leaves it again to pursue his course into infinity.

[51] From a poem, "Stosst an! Jena soll leben!" (Clink glasses! Jena shall live!), by August Binzer (1792-1868). Around 1818 it became popular with students and workers as a song of independence. (D. S.)

III

INAUGURAL ADDRESS, UPON ASSUMING THE CHAIRMANSHIP OF THE ZOFINGIA CLUB

(Winter Semester 1897/98)

Dear Friends:

143   It is customary for the newly elected chairman to deliver an inaugural address which paves his way to Hell with good intentions. Aware as I am of the arduous nature of my new office, I have come equipped with my own share of good intentions. Will I be able to put them into practice? I don't know, but let's hope for the best!

144   It would be tedious indeed for me to tell you about my good intentions. I believe that every one of us here respects every other so highly that he will automatically credit him with the intent to carry out his duties conscientiously. There is another topic far more worthy of discussion, namely that which it is the chairman's duty to represent: the Club. This is a subject whose dignity is second to none. So let us ask: How is our Zofingia faring?[1]

145   A superficial glance tells us that a group of fairly well-educated young men have formed a club, the Zofingia Club, which has branches in various Swiss towns. In this club we hear a lot about brotherhood, mutual understanding, allegiance to the club as a whole, the fact that we are making progress toward our common goals, and so on. On suitable occasions, which occur at least once a semester, we set off a lot of patriotic fireworks, which we seem to think very uplifting. From the outside the Zofingia looks solid and self-assured, a stone tower which, side by side with other stalwart towers that also serve an important function, is standing guard over a high-gabled old-world city. Therein live the merchants called "historical necessities." But in the center of the city towers a magnificent cathe-

---

[1] *Deleted:*

After all, the Zofingia is the alpha and omega of all our endeavors. The prosperity of the Club is the focal point of our concern.

To describe the present state of the Zofingia compared to what it was in the past is a task we may leave to historians. To describe the present state of the Zofingia compared to what it will be is a task we may leave to the moral philosopher. But to describe the state of the Zofingia today, without past, without future, purely in the present, is a task we may tacitly assume belongs among the duties of the newly-elected chairman.

dral, a place whither men of all times have made their pilgrimage. It is called "the Idea."

146 We can see the stone tower from far away. It is indeed solidly built, and many men without a country have banged their heads against it in vain, trying to break down the door.

147 Let us show no mercy, let us take a closer look. As we approach, our metaphor of the tower dissolves and blows away like mist, as all metaphors do. In vain we reach out for new metaphors, trying to capture in a single image all the refractory and irreconcilable features we see. But no metaphor fits, neither "whited sepulcher" nor that obstinate bundle of sticks which the goddess History has bound together with a red-and-white band.[2] Finding no appropriate metaphor, let's see what the reality is like. Let's take a look at the constitution, the only common intellectual denominator, the only thing that will rouse no opposition within the Club. With a pleasurable sense of trepidation, we open the venerable document. Alas, there on Page One, right beside Article 3, some German barbarian has left a dreadful inkblot!

148 We return to that elevated post from which we first gazed at the city. Indeed, it is not a bad view. The shopkeepers have hung out a lot of dirty historical linen, and a lot of foul business is being carried on in the narrow streets. But we see the roof of the pilgrims' church shining in the sunlight, and see how the grey towers and walls all guard the One Thing at the center. A thousand little fissures and cracks crisscross the masonry from the roof to the foundations, but the structure holds together.

149 We have found the right metaphor. All we were missing before was the "view from the top." But let's not get carried away. Let's come back to our own little club and see what's going on here. Are we too harboring, in our snug little hut, ill-concealed cracks where jackdaws and sparrows build their nests, which they seek to line to their own advantage? We can deny this in all good conscience. We have suffered no major damage. The floors here are a bit rotten, so that a number of people have already stumbled through and sprained their ankles.

150 The summer is not too hot, the winter not too cold; and in between there blow no bitter winds. In short, we are in a position to offer a snug hostel to people who are not too particular. And

[2] Red and white are the colors of the Swiss flag, here binding the fascicles of the Swiss cantons.

they often take us up on our offer of hospitality, so that one is inclined to feel that the tone of the place is almost a little too easygoing. Let us beware, for there's a raw wind blowing outside and life is not going to give us a free ride.

151   The Zofingia has set itself the task of forming its members into responsible citizens who work for progress in all areas of political and social life. Born in an age of political storm and stress, maturing amid the manifold vicissitudes of political thought in the mid-nineteenth century, the Zofingia has now come to rest in the tranquil, perhaps even languid waves of a port: the port of political and philanthropic endeavor. Now and then people point to some outstanding politician and say that the Zofingia Club has done its job well. I am inclined to doubt this. We have not achieved the ideal we dreamed of. Hundreds of alumni have left the active ranks of the Zofingia without ever having displayed the least enthusiasm for a political idea. Among them were men of high reputation in Switzerland. To be sure, it is a testament to our high-mindedness that we set ourselves an unattainable ideal, but the day may come when our members are compelled to soberly ask themselves: Is it really our mission to chase after some brightly-colored soap bubble called "historical necessity," to capture a beautiful but unattainable rainbow? The day may come when, aghast and filled with doubt, we will ask ourselves: Ought we really to devote our most ardent enthusiasm to the historical idea of a fatherland? Are we to place our greatest skills in the service of some political movement we have decided has merit? Now we can still dream of good times to come, but for how much longer can we do so? Nowadays we don't know what political upheavals are anymore. The spring storm of political zeal has long since died away in the skies above our blasé age. A terrifying lassitude is making itself felt everywhere, as is evident if we merely consider the miserable participation in our plebiscites. What would a man like Abel Burckhardt[3] have said to all this? The newspapers are doing their part to heighten our lassitude, disgust,

---

[3] In the holograph Jung first wrote Jakob Burckhardt, then altered the first name to Abel.

Abel Burckhardt (1805-1882), the first Basel section chairman, composed the song "Was brausest du mein junges Blut." A member of Zofingia since 1823, a student of theology and a pastor, he gave many lectures exhorting his comrades to show courage and to lead an inner religious life. See *Centralblatt des Schweizerischen Zofingervereins*, XXIII:3 (Jan. 1883), 110ff. (M.-L. v. F.) Another Abel Burckhardt (1871-1958), also a pastor, was a Zofingia comrade of Jung's.

and ennui. Unspeakably vile machinations, shabby intrigues, vilifications, imputations, the filthiest insinuations, the filthiest trash that a filthy journalist hack can invent: These are the stock-in-trade of the press, which daily stirs up the rabble and drives away the educated man. This kind of thing takes place in every party, no matter how conservative. Even if, out of consideration for the moral attitudes of readers, decent newspapers do not print what is downright vile, they manage to achieve the ultimate in sheer triviality. That's the way things are in our dear fatherland. Outside Switzerland, in the realm of international politics, things are much the same, only it's all done on a grander scale. If a decent fellow from some planet where there is no such thing as politics, were suddenly to drop down on the earth and see what has been done to Crete and Greece;[4] how all the world's potentates are creeping to the Mongol prince on the Neva and trying to outdo each other in paying him honor a posteriori; and how the German Kaiser is cosying up to the wild boar of Turkey, he would heartily agree with the refreshing words of old Blücher:[5] "They are damned bastards, those diplomats!"

152   The true nature of politics is becoming clearer all the time. It is a desolate naked picture indeed, a grimace too sad to be amusing.

153   Where are those beings born of fire and the spirit, the champions of a creative idea? Where are those men who reach their mighty hands into the spokes of the universal wheel, and who carve new channels to guide the surge of half-formed ideas? They are a thing of the past, and so are the inspired thoughts to which they gave birth.

154   No doubt a few optimists among us will protest and passionately maintain that modern man has not ceased to display a sacred zeal for political causes. I admit that here and there we find little groups of two or three comrades who display genuine political enthusiasms. But as a rule the mass enthusiasms of today are preeminently stupid

4 In 1896 the Cretans rebelled against Turkish rule and in 1897 declared Crete united with Greece, which sent troops to assist the rebels. The Greco-Turkish War, or Thirty Days' War, of 1897, resulted in the overwhelming defeat of the Greeks by the Turkish army, which had been reorganized under German supervision. Greece yielded to the pressure of the European powers, withdrew its troops from Crete, was forced to pay Turkey an indemnity, and yielded territory in Thessaly to Turkey.

5 Gebhard Leberecht von Blücher, prince of Wahlstatt, (1742-1819), field marshal who led Prussian armies in victories over Napoleon, 1813-1815.

affairs. For example, just recall the sacred ardor of the Langenthal Radicals[6] who, when asked to vote on the looting raid business, voted a thunderous "No" with great fanfare. Or the edifying moments in our own marketplace when, because he was suffering from a catarrh, Herr Brenner was unable to salute his loyal gymnasts' and schoolmasters' clubs. As a rule there is always a newspaper reporter present on such occasions, and near him some venerable old man who, overcome by emotion, is compelled to wipe his eyes continually, and who solemnly deposes that he has never before experienced anything so beautiful and uplifting, even though he is already old and has lived through the separatist war and the Prussian negotiations.

155   Even more inane are the official displays of public enthusiasm in the pan-German Empire; but most inane of all are the French demonstrations of zeal regarding the Russians.

156   Only one of the splendid demonstrations of political conviction that we have witnessed in recent times is that which fired up the Greeks to fight the Turks. It really warmed one's heart to see it. Then the official political rabble-rousers from all over Europe rushed to pluck the young eagle's feathers in order to help ensure the victory of everything unlawful, vile, dissolute, stupid, and trivial.

157   The Zofingia demands that we send competent politicians out into this chaos. What is a competent politician? Is he a *homo politicus*, a particular type of human being without soul and conscience? Apparently that is the kind of politician we need if he is to be forced to wade through the river of political mud. Fortunately such people cannot be made but are born, born out of the unfathomable womb of time, two or three of them every century. These men *must* do what they are born for. The nations bless them and revere them as saints, or curse them as the scourges of God. The Zofingia cannot make such men. It strives to make good citizens, *homunculi politici* (political men on a modest scale). But these good citizens need to have a soul and a conscience, if only to provide a foil for the great men, they need to provide a source of friction against which the great can rub themselves as against pieces of flint until their spirits

---

[6] In 1850, the new Zofingians and Helvetians postulated that the old conservative Zofingians should not be invited to the annual meeting. When the local authorities of Zofingen did not agree, the new Zofingians chose the town of Langenthal as meeting place. See Werner Kundert, *Abriss der Geschichte des Schweizerischen Zofingervereins* (Lausanne, 1961), p. 21. (M.-L. v. F.)

flame up and give off thunder and lightning. And perhaps they are needed too to promote progress, to serve as the champions and propagators of new ideas. The great man bombards the world with problems and tasks, indifferent as to whether these are productive or destructive. But the Zofingia Club is here to help ensure that there will be human beings in the world to respond to new problems and tasks, human beings in the true sense of the word. The Zofingia must form human, not political animals, human beings who laugh and weep, human beings conscious of their minds and wills, human beings who know that they are living among other human beings and that they must all put up with each other because they are all condemned to be human. A task like this is enough to drive one to despair, for it is nothing less than that of cleaning the Augean stables, trying to break down this towering mountain of rubbish which has maliciously insinuated itself between man and man. Let us take a really good look at this mission of ours! It is sublime, for it embraces everything that we humans have to do on earth. It is the task of raising up both ourselves and our neighbors.

158   There are many ways to achieve this goal. I consider the noblest to be that of unsparing intellectual interchange, free from all prejudice and from all secondary motives; the way of learning to know man as man and not as some lovable form of social livestock. Such genuine exchange will prevent us from judging by appearances, from judging by the surface. It will enable us to forge bonds of friendship which do justice to the word *amicitia* in our motto. It will pave the way to the *litteris*, to the education, which no university any longer supplies. Oh if only things were still as they used to be, when men walked up and down in the cool courts of Athens. . . .

159   When we step out into the world of everyday life, we will find there a citizen who is able to live up to the motto of his student days: *patriae*.

160   As for drinking, that much-maligned and misconstrued pastime which has become the hallmark of the university student, can we not ennoble our drinking bouts and turn them into a real *symposium*?

161   It is your task and mine to promote intellectual communion. This task is high but not beyond reach, and it is our duty to carry it out. We should always do our duty. For, Nietzsche notwithstanding, there is something to morality after all.

162   My "confession" is now at an end.

IV

THOUGHTS ON THE NATURE AND VALUE OF SPECULATIVE INQUIRY

(Summer 1898)

INTRODUCTION

Auditoribus meis mortuis, semi mortuis, semi vivis, vivis.

(To my audience, dead, half dead, half alive, alive.)

163 "Thoughts on the nature and value of speculative inquiry?" muse the members of my gracious audience. "No doubt it's just more nonsense from the fourth dimension dressed up in flowery philosophical language."[1] Oh, but you don't know how wrong you are! Now "as the bottle flows darkly we'll hear a bituminous song"! My talk will contain no wild speeches blaspheming the dear saints who reign over the cult of matter; no revolutionary campaigns against traditional truths; no crushing boulders thundering out of my tainted heritage; nothing of the kind! I will trot around, scrupulously objective, like a little pony, meek as a lamb, minding my p's and q's and bridled like a good burgher, carrying the orthodox staff of the city of Basel on my back. There will not be the slightest trace of that frightfully coarse child of nature. My words will be sweet as pie, and caressed by gentle zephyrs, as if we were having high tea on a family outing of the League of Virtue.

164 My talk will be free of all corrosive subjectivity, scrupulously objective, stripped of everything personal like a shirt that has been taken off, washed, pleated, and ironed. Its general tenor will be stilted and tedious, but for the sake of ideas, I have cunningly interlarded my discourse with two quotations per page, "maxims from good authors" which every young university student would do well to act upon. What I have to say will be lengthy and boring like every good big discussion topic. As a rule an ideal address to the Zofingia Club is related to one of our three mottoes. Thus we hear talks about federal banks, folk songs, fraternity brothers, and freshmen. My paper relates to all three mottoes. In other words,

---

[1] *Inserted marginally as a "note for [sic] the author"*: Now, wanderer, get a move on, or he'll pull your leg!

59

it is a cubic lecture to the Zofingia circle. (Note for the author.) So, as I have said, it is all as it should be.

165   But some people may perhaps think just the opposite, depending on how they feel about science and scientific research:

> To one man she is the exalted, celestial goddess, to the other a sturdy cow which provides him with butter.
>
> Schiller[2]

[2] Friedrich Schiller, *Xenien*, "Wissenschaft," No. 62 of *Musenalmanach für das Jahr 1797*, p. 316, in *Werke*, Vol. I, *Gedichte* 1776-1799 (Weimar, 1945).

THOUGHTS ON THE NATURE AND VALUE OF
SPECULATIVE INQUIRY

> *quid aeternis minorem*
> *consiliis animum fatigas?*
>
> (Why do you weary yourself about
> a future that is eternal and so
> cannot be known?)
> —Horace, Ode XI, Book II

166   Kant says somewhere that philosophy and the sciences are intellectual luxuries. Just now it is particularly important for us to
give some thought to this significant remark, for in today's world
people are inclined to pursue scientific work for the sake of success,
and to judge all scientific activities in these terms. They evaluate
their field of study in terms of its future income, and as a rule it
is thought better to avoid any digression from their prescribed plan
of study. Why? Because digressions, raids into other fields, reap
no profit. In other words, excursions into outlying territory do not
enable one to achieve any advantage over competitors in one's own
field. Indeed, such excursions actually dissipate one's energies and
tend to impede one's progress in the field. Thus digressions are a
luxury which many can ill afford. But Kant says that every science
is a luxury. A luxury is something that is not useful. Strictly speaking, no science is the least bit useful. The uncivilized peoples of
the world all testify to the fact that man can survive perfectly well
without science. Science is not useful until it abandons its exalted
status as a goal in itself and sinks to the level of an industry. The
civilized peoples of every age have striven unceasingly to strip science of its pervasive uselessness and to make it serve practical ends.
For to man in his natural state, a thing that cannot be used is nothing
at all, and an activity that produces no tangible result is not an
activity. This is why the farmer and the salesman generally regard
the scholar as an idle parasite. The noblest of all the sciences,

philosophy, is now afflicted on a grand scale by that same contempt that has always plagued it on a small scale. Every industrialist, whether he is a businessman or a factory owner, a chemist or a physician,[3] judges all endeavors that do not produce tangible results, as useless—and because they are useless, as downright injurious.[4] The infinitely practical and wholly realistic trend of our age is averse to all idealism. The focal point of concern has been shifted to the relations between external things. People feel that the salvation of the human race consists in well-ordered states, in social development. They view the happiness of the individual as determined by external circumstances—for example, by financial security. So it is no wonder if everything is adapted to this purpose. In certain fields the secularization of human interests has proved extraordinarily productive. First, we have it to thank for the development of our culture in general. It gave rise to the smooth-fitting structure of the modern nation-state, and it is the source of every practical technological and industrial advance achieved by the sciences. Human beings, intoxicated by the pleasures of material success, are throwing themselves into the bustle and tumult of existence. They hope that material success will give them everything. It is only logical that this trend, more pronounced in our time than in any previous age, should also bring to light some remarkable paradoxes. We cannot abstain from mentioning a few. For example, nationalism, the total devotion to the state, social democracy. Even the church (*situm teneamus!*—Let us keep our places!), is joining the roundelay and manifesting all sorts of curious traits. In the churches people pray for the welfare of the fatherland, but apparently remain oblivious of the fact that every social benefit must necessarily be compensated by some social misfortune. Thus indirectly we pray that foreign manufacturers may suffer disaster so that our own industry can derive some benefit from it. Indeed, the representatives of the modern Christian church have gone so far as to preach devotion to the state, and regard the church as the institution responsible for the formation of good citizens. Nietzsche has said: "Here we see the results of that doctrine which in recent days has been preached from all the rooftops, that the state is the highest goal of mankind and that a man has no higher duty than to serve

3 *Deleted*: a jurist or a social reformer.
4 *Deleted*: When anyone rises above the norm, everyone asks: "Well, what's he good for? Whom is he profiting?"

the state. I regard this as a reversion not to paganism but to stupidity."[5]

167 The concept of the secularization of all human concerns has also laid hold on philosophical circles and has found its champions there—for example, Eduard von Hartmann with his immanent and eudaemonistic moral principle. There is also Wilhelm Max Wundt, the advocate of humanistic goals.

168 Material success has not always been man's sole aim. The Middle Ages saw the flowering of the idea of the theocratic state, and thousands of cloisters and churches testified to the fact that the focal point of existence lay not in external phenomena but in the inner life of each individual human being. Man was in much closer touch with nature, and was not hemmed into superficial relationships by the thousand amenities of civilized life. He found the time to be an individual among individuals. The basic principle of his civilization was concern with the world's future. In other words, medieval man regarded material success as of little or no importance. For him development represented an internal, not an external problem. He knew nothing of the concept of common welfare, of social prosperity. All he understood was that the world could be improved and redeemed through the development and improvement of the individual. Medieval man was characterized by a transcendental egotism. Modern man is characterized by an immanent egotism. There is no need to point out which is the Christian point of view. Modern man knows nothing of the individual. The individuals he knows are cantons and nation-states. As a rule he has already lost his consciousness of himself as an individual. He feels that he is an atom, a mere link in the endless chain that makes up the state. Modern man shifts responsibility for the creation of individual happiness from himself to the state, i.e., to the legally regulated relations between himself and his fellow men. Differences between individuals involve a difference in their requirements. Such differences lead to nuisances affecting the lawful unity and homogeneity of the state, and thus modern man seeks to level, that is, to wipe out, individuality by educating everyone, as much as possible, to be exactly the same. Nowadays, it is not

[5] *Unzeitgemässe Betrachtungen* ("Untimely Reflections"), Kröner Taschenausgabe, vol. 71, p. 230.

true that each man is the architect of his own fortune; instead the state creates his fortune for the individual.

169   The absolute secularization of all concerns is the characteristic that distinguishes modern from medieval man.

170   The process of perfecting external relations has torn man away from his bond with nature, but only from the conscious bond, not from the unconscious. Civilized man believes that he has risen sky-high above the crudities of nature. For twenty or thirty years he actually *is* a privy councilor of His Excellency Prince So-and-So, or a member of the Swiss representative assembly, and so on. But overnight comes some treacherous bacterium, and all the glory of civilized man within the best-ordered nation in the world, super-ficially so splendid, is suddenly lying there sick and wretched, no better and no worse than any Hottentot or our ancestors the trog-lodytes. What help, then, is the whole civilized world, what use is the magnificent future one's grandchildren have to look forward to in which, thanks to our technological progress, they will travel in airships and eat synthetic protein? Poor old civilized man, no matter how civilized and politically up-to-date he may have been, has been abandoned by life and, yielding to its pitiless decree, must leave behind an existence to which he had given his deepest ap-proval and affirmation. He has achieved material success, but did it make him happy? No, of course not. There is no pleasure in having things, but only in obtaining them. Never has anyone achieved such success that he did not want more. The reason for this is simply that man strives for happiness, which remains happiness only for the moment he achieves it, but which afterwards reverts to the same old insipid round he knew before. The fact that modern man seeks happiness in material success causes him to reject as ineffectual any endeavor that is not directed toward this single end. The assumption that happiness lies in external factors is for the most part an a priori judgment, i.e., most people do not have the slightest inkling that happiness could consist in anything else. They never conceive, as it were, that well-being could be based on some-thing other than external causes. But this is a totally erroneous conclusion. To be sure, the conclusion is founded on what appears to be an accurate piece of inductive reasoning, in that people see that material success gives one a feeling of pleasure. This obser-vation leads to the false notion: Material success is the cause of all joy and must, under all circumstances, make people happy. Success

is not necessarily organically linked to joy. In itself it is totally neutral. Everything depends on the individual. If he is already happy, success will increase his happiness. If he is unhappy, even the most spectacular success may often awaken feelings of great bitterness. Happiness is purely subjective and bears no necessary relationship to anything external. If this were not true, everyone who did not have a million francs would be unhappy in direct proportion to the square of his distance from this goal. Happiness is so subjective that frequently it is entirely independent of external factors. As Goethe says, "You have not gained refreshment / If it does not flow out of your own soul."[6]

171   Thus we see that modern man's striving for happiness is extremely one-sided in that we seek happiness in inessential, accidental causes external to ourselves. But Schopenhauer long ago established that happiness external to ourselves is not really happiness at all but only the cessation of unhappiness. Thus in our search for positive happiness we are entirely dependent on our own resources, that is, on subjective factors. Nowhere outside ourselves is there any positive happiness, for positive happiness is a subjective state whose causes lie wholly outside the objective chain of cause and effect. Thus the road to happiness does not lead through the theaters and concert halls, or through honor and glory, but rather up or down into the unfathomable depths of our own being. Schopenhauer says: "For behind our existence lies something else which becomes accessible to us only when we have put aside the world." One factor of positive happiness is a so-called good conscience, i.e., the feeling of moral blamelessness. This feeling derives from the gratification of an instinctive impulse that Kant called the categorical imperative. It is the irrepressible demand to do what we regard as good, and refrain from doing what we regard as morally evil. It gives us a feeling of pleasure to act in accordance with the requirements of the categorical imperative, just as the gratification of any instinct brings with it a certain quantity of pleasure. In recent times Eduard von Hartmann has attached particular importance to this sense of pleasure arising from the gratification of instinct, and has documented it, using inductive logic, from countless scientific examples. Another inexhaustible source of happiness can be the gratification of the causal instinct. Just as, in the

[6] *Faust I*, "Night," lines 568-569.

field of practical reason, *one* vote and *one* law governs our action, so in the realm of pure reason we are ruled by *one* law whence all scientific laws are derived—the category of causality. When Kant was investigating the laws governing human thought, he found that all thought unfolds within the confines of certain forms that he called categories. He found twelve such categories. In his critique of Kantian philosophy, Schopenhauer reduced the number to three— time, space, and causality. Time and space are forms of perception, and causality is a form of thought. These three are a priori categories, i.e., they are judgments prior to experience. The mind cannot function without them, for there is no such thing as a mental image that does not unfold within the structure of time and space, and there is no such thing as a thought process whose innermost nature is not causality. The need for causal thinking is innate in virtually every human being, but is particularly developed in those with philosophical minds. The gratification of the need for causal thinking is called truth. Most probably it is impossible, in the light of critical reason, to achieve total knowledge of the causes involved in the concept of truth. But it makes no difference to our happiness whether the truth we perceive is absolute or completely relative, for the gratification of our need to think causally is proportional not to the truth value of our cognition but to the degree of faith we ascribe to it. Almost certainly all our knowledge is highly relative, but our belief that it is absolute makes us blissfully happy.

172   It is the gratification of two a priori requirements—the categorical imperative and the category of causality—that, under certain circumstances, makes a person happy and gives him a feeling of contentment which no external factor can confer. The frail and transitory nature of all the external factors in human life is so apparent that there is no need to discuss it. A man can survive all his friends and relatives, bury what he loves most and lead a lonely existence as a stranger in an alien time; but he cannot survive himself and the inner factors of his life, and cannot bury them, for they are his very self, and thus are inalienable.

173   Someone might raise the objection that, despite their instability, factors external to the person do—at least for as long as they last— constitute a source of positive happiness. But apart from the fact that this kind of happiness appears to many people to be contemptible, it should be noted that with respect to pleasure or the lack of it, external relationships are more or less neutral, and that

everything depends on the person's subjective disposition. The most magnificent landscape, the most divine music, are nothing but a wisp of smoke if a man is suffering from toothache. There is an inner disposition suitable to every external pleasure, whether that disposition is health or peace of mind.

174   From what we have said so far, it is clear that there are two kinds of happiness, one authentic and enduring, the other merely apparent and highly unstable. Of course, the only person who can really appreciate the implications of this truth is one who has already milked his happiness for all it is worth, has asked from it everything it has to give. This truth is familiar to malcontents, who have already moved heaven and earth trying to obtain the happiness they crave. The contented man, the satisfied man, is not competent to judge of these matters. (Note for the author.) In the final analysis the striving for happiness can be described as the motivation for every human act. But man does not live alone, nor is it good that a man should be alone. His fellow men crave happiness from him just as they do from all others. It is in order to gratify this desire that men invented the state, the mechanism that absorbs the successes of the individual and then redistributes them, in a diluted form, to all the members of the confederation. But the state, as the totality of all its citizens, can utilize only material successes, and thus clearly value can be attributed only to the striving for material success. Thus the happiness of the individual must also possess objectivity, that is, it must derive from an objectively perceptible source. If such a source cannot be produced, as is the case with purely ideal happiness, then it is concluded that the striving for ideal ends is without value. At this point we confront a new question: Do philosophy and pure science really represent an intellectual luxury in the transcendental sense, and can metaphysical reality be attributed to the as yet ideal goal of gratifying the need to think in causal terms?[7]

175   Radical subjectivists, i.e., those who regard the world as illusion, and multiplicity as a show of glittering nothingness, deny any objectivity of purpose. That is, they do not acknowledge the existence of any teleology external to man, and instead claim that we ourselves have projected onto the world, out of our own heads, the idea of the purposefulness of nature. At least the epigones of Kant

[7] *Deleted*: and the categorical imperative?

have this much in common with the materialists. Obviously this viewpoint is extremely barren and unproductive. It means certain death to any speculative inquiry based on an inductive, scientific method. It means despair to any healthy person of heart and sensibility. All philosophy must have an empirical foundation. The only true basis for philosophy is what we experience of ourselves and, through ourselves, of the world around us. Every a priori structure that converts our experience into an abstraction must inevitably lead us to erroneous conclusions. By now we ought to know this, having observed the lapses of the first post-Kantian philosophers such as Fichte, Schelling, and Hegel. As Nietzsche says, our philosophy should, first and foremost, be a philosophy of what lies nearest to hand. Our philosophy should consist in drawing inferences about the unknown, in accordance with the principle of sufficient reason, on the basis of *real experience*, and not in drawing inferences about the inner world on the basis of the outer, or denying external reality by affirming only the inner world. Apart from the eight[8] a priori categories of time, space, and causality,[9] there is none that is not based on experience. Thus judgments about purpose are not a priori judgments, for the objectivity of a priori judgments cannot be demonstrated. But according to the principle of sufficient reason, it is possible to demonstrate purposes external to ourselves. Eduard von Hartmann was the first to do this, and he did it using a method drawn from exact science, namely by the calculation of probability.

176   Any act can be designated as purposeful if it is based on an objective notion of purpose. According to the principle of sufficient reason, a notion of purpose must exist prior to every action intended to have a purposeful character. Every human being has had subjective experience of the accuracy of this principle. If we observe another person perform a purposeful action, we infer, by comparing what we have observed with our own deliberate actions, that this person had a definite intention in mind. A posteriori confirmation is supplied through the testimony of the person himself. It tells us that our inference, based on analogy, was correct. If we summarize thousands and thousands of correct inferences, we arrive at inductive proof of the objectivity of a purpose. We

[8] As holograph. Error for "three"? But cf n. 9.
[9] *Deleted*: the categorical imperative and the positive instincts.

have no notion about other purposeful actions which are not pre-
ceded by a purposeful intention, unless the action in question is
instinctive. It is characteristic of an instinctive action that each of
the steps that make it up must necessarily be purposeful, and its
outcome the best possible. To elucidate instinctive action, it is ad-
visable that we recall Newton's almost forgotten *Regulae philoso-
phandi*: The *Regula secunda* states: "Ideoque effectuum naturalium
eiusdem generis eandem assignandae sunt causae, quatenus fieri
potest. (Uti respirationis in homine et in bestia; descensus lapidum
in Europa et in America; lucis in igne culinari et in sole; reflexionis
lucis in terra et in planetis.)"[10]

177   According to this rule of Newton, we must refrain from creating
any new principle to explain instinctive action, and instead infer,
on the basis of already-existing experience, the existence of a purposeful intention which is unknown to us and not directly demon-
strable, and which underlies every instinctive action. Thus we can
say: An instinctive action is an action whose cause can be material,
i.e., tangible, but whose true motivation is a purposeful idea which
is unknown to us.[11]

178   Instinct is an agent which, without being subject to our will,
influences our actions, or rather modifies them in a direction of
which we are not consciously aware, and which is only recognized
a posteriori. By this definition the category of causality can be
designated an instinct. Helmholtz says in his book on the physiological theory of optics: "Thus the principle of sufficient reason is
really nothing other than the impulse of our mind to subject all
our perceptions to its governance; it is not a law of nature."[12] It is
not difficult to prove this assertion. The most primitive form of

---

[10] "Rule II: Therefore to the same natural effects we must, as far as possible, assign
the same cause. (As to respiration in a man and in a beast; the descent of stones in
Europe and in America; the light of our culinary fire and of the sun; the reflection
of light in the earth, and in the planets.)" Issac Newton, *Principles of Natural Philosophy
and His System of the World* (Berkeley, 1946), p. 398.

[11] *Deleted*: Eduard von Hartmann established this with a proof based on probability
theory.

   The German philosopher Hartmann (1842-1906) was influenced by Hegel and
Schopenhauer. In his later writings, Jung often cited Hartmann's *Philosophie des
Unbewussten* (Philosophy of the Unconscious), 1869, and other works.

[12] Hermann von Helmholtz, *A Treatise on Physiological Optics* (orig. 1867; tr., New
York, Dover reprint, 1961), Vol. IV, par. 26, "Concerning the Perceptions in General," pp. 30-31.

causation is found in unconscious inferences. If our peripheral nerve-ends are stimulated and the stimulus enters our consciousness in the form of a sensation, the idea of an external cause must also be present, i.e., we immediately and unconsciously relate the stimulus to an external cause. Thus independently of the cooperation of our will, the causal instinct has anticipated what in time may become a conscious thought process—namely the link to an external cause. The linking occurs on an unconscious level, quite independently of the will, and the result is delivered to us ready-made, as if it came from outside us.

179   Like other instincts such as love, the instinctive need to think in causal terms is manifested in weaker and stronger forms. Under certain circumstances the primitive form of the instinct to think causally can become so powerful that it can take over all intellectual functions and modify them to suit itself. Just as the sexual drive frequently transforms man into a monster, so the elementary category of causality can assume the character of a need, an insatiable craving which overruns everything, and which people will even sacrifice their lives to gratify. It is an indefatigable longing which inflames us, which makes us despise all the works and ordinances of man, which makes us smile when others are weeping. (Note for the author.) It is that ardent desire for truth which impetuously breaks down all barriers and is even capable of crushing the will to live. It is a good story, if an apocryphal one, that Empedocles leaped into the crater of Mount Etna in order to fathom the unfathomable. To be sure, Horace imputes to him other motives, motives that are quite consistent with the character of a Roman:

> Deus immortalis haberi
> dum cupit Empedocles, ardentem frigidus Aetnam
> insiluit.[13]

180   But it is not only in classical antiquity that we find such figures, expressive of the genuinely tragic spirit, such Faustian beings whose life and death lies in the knowledge of truth. When Heinrich von Kleist had read Kant's critique of epistemology, he wrote to a friend: "The truth which we amass here, ceases to exist after death, and all effort to win something of our own which will follow us into the grave, is vain.—If the point of this thought fails to pierce your

[13] Horace, *Ars poetica*, lines 464-466: "Desiring to be considered an immortal god, Empedocles leaped in cold blood into fiery Etna."

heart, then do not smile at another who feels himself deeply wounded in his most sacred and innermost part. My sole, my highest goal has been lost and I have no other."[14]

181   In every healthy, reflective person the simple need to satisfy the principle of causality develops into a metaphysical longing, into religion. When the first man asked: Why? and tried to investigate the reason for some change, science was born. But science alone does not satisfy anyone. It must be expanded into what DeWitte calls a philosophy "full of faith and enthusiasm, which alone merits the exalted name of wisdom."[15] Every genuine philosophy, as the complete expression of metaphysical desire, is religion. Religion is the mother who receives her children with loving arms when they flee to her terrified by the confusion and the "merciless tumult of nature stripped of its gods," and driven to despair by the shattering enigma of existence.

182   We use the term "instinctive actions" to designate all those incomparably wondrous and purposeful actions on the part of plants and animals which have justly aroused the awe of all scientists. Particularly at the beginning of this century, many outstanding thinkers displayed the keenest interest in instinct. Thus Schelling says: "The manifestations of animal instinct are among the most impressive known to any thoughtful man, and are the true touchstone of genuine philosophy." Charles Darwin actually felt obliged to install instinct as a new principle in his theory of evolution.[16] As we know, Schopenhauer describes instinct as a stage in the objectification of the Will. So does Hartmann, adding the absolutely essential element of the purposeful intention.

183   Absolute purposefulness is the hallmark of all instinctive actions. As we have demonstrated, the category of causality should be regarded as an instinct. Thus the instinct to satisfy causality is also absolutely purposeful.[17]

[14] Cf. Kleist's letter to his sister Ulrike von Kleist, dated Berlin, 23 March 1801.
[15] Probably Wilhelm Martin Leberecht de Wette (1780-1849), professor of theology at Berlin until 1822, when his radical rationalism provoked his dismissal. Thereafter he was professor at Basel. Jung's library contains his *Das Wesen des christlichen Glaubens vom Standpunkt des Glaubens dargestellt* (1846).
[16] *Deleted*: This procedure can be explained only by the well-known casualness of certain scientists with regard to the just requirements of logic.
[17] *Deleted*: Thus the category of causality is to be viewed as a wondrous a priori indication . . .

184   If we backtrack along a chain of cause and effect, we soon arrive at a limit where our understanding—i.e., our ability to tabulate ideas of tangible causes—ceases to function. Physics furnishes an excellent example. A stone falls to the ground. Why? Because of gravity. Why does it respond to gravity? Because it is its property to do so. At this point our ability to grasp the situation comes to an end. We posit the, in itself, incomprehensible principle of universal gravitation, i.e., we set up a transcendental postulate. Causality leads us to a *Ding an sich* for which we cannot account further, to a cause whose nature is transcendental. In this sense the category of causality must be interpreted as a totally wondrous a priori reference to causes of a transcendental nature, i.e., to a world of the invisible and incomprehensible, a continuation of material nature into the incalculable, the immeasurable, and the inscrutable. Surely it is unnecessary for me to add that such an interpretation places the doctrine of the *Ding an sich* in a new light and enables us to get an unexpected glimpse of the superb purposefulness of the animate universe.

185   Let us return to the question we posed before: Does the initially ideal purpose of the need to satisfy causality possess metaphysical reality? The foregoing discussion reveals that we have, with sufficient reason, demonstrated the existence of purpose. If the a priori status of the principle of causation has a purpose, then it also has a use—but the use is transcendental just like the purpose. The purpose underlying causality points far beyond our present existence, and justifies the hopes we cherish, of producing an infinite chain of effects attended by infinite success. But be that as it may, causality has purpose, and thus science, philosophy, and religion also have a use—a transcendental use. Hence the whole pack of those who disparage the gratification of the need for causal thinking on the grounds that it is useless, are completely wrong. Let them bark away! We can console ourselves with Goethe's thought:

> The loud peal of their barks
> simply proves that we are riding high![18]

186   The fact that we do not recognize the purpose, the fact that this purpose is still wholly ideal, does not matter in the least. If a bird

---

[18] These lines from Goethe's poem "Kläffer," No. 190 of his *Sprüche* (1808), describe the derisive barking or yelping of the pack which pursues us in all our endeavors. Properly they read "Und seines Bellens lauter Schall / Beweist nur, dass wir reiten."

raised in captivity, far from his own kind, is overcome by wanderlust in the autumn, does he know that winter will soon settle over the land and that he will die in misery of the cold and hunger? Is his wanderlust unpurposeful because its purpose is hidden from the conscious mind? But as human beings we should know that now it is autumn and that a winter is coming from whose terrors a sound instinct is warning us to flee. Nietzsche states, in an exquisite passage: "A winter day is upon us, and we live in poverty and danger on high mountains. Brief is every joy and pale every gleam of sunlight which steals down to us on the white mountains."

187   The need to satisfy the law of causality accompanies us everywhere like a faithful shepherd, and we never cease to hear its voice. Each time we confront some question, does it not step into our path, pleading with us and encouraging us: "Yes, ask, go on and on asking questions, in the end you must reach your goal!" Does it not challenge us to halt on the path and, overcome by doubt, to say: "What was I yesterday, what am I today, what will I be tomorrow? Toward what goal am I striving, toward what goal does the universe tend? What is the purpose of the starry sky with its countless worlds which whirl and swirl on their paths for millions of years? Why do we not heed the slightest stirrings of genius? Why do we not stretch out our hands toward the never-fading flowers whose fragrance alleviates our every pain? Again and again we allow ourselves to be dazzled by the fleeting success of the moment, afraid to set out on the path which leads into the flooding mist."

188   "The world about us is full of ghostly doings," says Nietzsche. "Every moment of our lives is trying to tell us something, but we do not care to listen to this spirit voice. When we are alone and still, we are afraid that something will be whispered in our ears, and so we hate the stillness and anesthetize ourselves through sociability."

189   We place too much trust in this world, we believe too firmly in the happiness to be derived from success, despite the fact that the greatest of all men, Christ and the sages of all ages, teach and demonstrate that we should do just the opposite. We reject every metaphysical desire with Schiller's words: "Do you know what awaits you there? What a high price you are paying? That you are trading a certain good for one that is uncertain? Do you feel you have enough strength to wage the most difficult war? When mind and

73

heart, feeling and thought, do not agree, have you courage enough to sing along with the immortal hydra of doubt? And to manfully confront the enemy in yourself?"

190   We, on the other hand, say: Nothing ventured, nothing gained. A person who bases his happiness on things external to himself may see his whole world crumble overnight. Everything external to ourselves can change. Everything that we are in relation to others can vanish away. What is a king without his royal household and his lands? What is a general without soldiers? What is a dignitary without people to acknowledge his position? All external success and external prestige can and one day will crumble away. But no one can take from us our *inward* achievements, for they stand and fall with our own being. People can lock a Socrates in an underground prison, blind him, cut out his tongue, but he remains Socrates, and the wealth and abundance of his mind belongs to him and will remain his, inalienable and unfading, for as long as he exists.

191   The instinctive need to satisfy causality, as an a priori reference to transcendental causes, constitutes religion. It is the infinitely subtle agent that frees man from his animal nature, raises him to the plane of science and philosophy, and thence carries him off into infinity. And yet it is instinct. This realization leads us to a new train of thought, to a new and complex problem. The question is: What is the relation between the causal instinct and the other instincts, and whence do we derive the justification for giving precedence to the causal instinct?

192   Up to now we have justified the gratification of the need to satisfy the law of causality, on the grounds that it is the source of the greatest happiness. But we have also demonstrated that happiness is invariably a purely subjective state, and so our line of reasoning constitutes nothing more than an *argumentum ad hominem*. Now we must supplement it with an *argumentum ad rem*.

193   This new challenge leads us far onto the infinite battlefield of philosophical world views.

> Through a twilight between dawns
> the path of men leads to the field of the dead.
> They go to sleep weary
> of the indulgence and chastisement of the Powers.

194   So says Lucas Heland:[19] a twilight, a pale gleam, a struggle between day and night—that is human life. The man of reflection is
dismayed and confused by the alien, unfathomable, restless bustle
of a thing he has not made, which does not exist for his sake, a
thing that pursues itself in a thousand forms, indifferent to the
existence of a man vainly wrestling with philosophical perplexities
and trying to confer a meaning on it all, to find "the point of rest
amid the flight of appearances."[20] Sometimes it seems to him that
everything has been created to live, that every atom is struggling
to express vitality in motion. But behold! All the splendid blossoms
that a benevolent spring sunshine has summoned into luxuriant
life and growth, fall victim overnight to the malevolent frost, and
in the morning the flower of life has been broken and its roots
destroyed. Then the man thinks: Everything has been created for
a brief hour, only to plunge into the eternal night of death. But
behold! New life springs from every death; glowing life bursts forth
again and again with inexhaustible energy. For life is in fact an
eternal flux: $\pi\acute{\alpha}\nu\tau\alpha\ \dot{\rho}\varepsilon\tilde{\imath}$,[21] there is an unceasing coming-into-being
and passing away, an ever-changing profusion without meaning or
purpose, each successive surge of life more absurd than the last, a
mad carnival show that nature puts on, to the pain of the thoughtful
man. This solution to the world's riddle gives no satisfaction, for
man desires the gratification of his need to perceive a purposeful
relation between cause and effect. Man wants to know why and
what for, just as he wants his own actions and those of his fellow
men to have a purpose. Man is a Prometheus who steals lightning
from heaven in order to bring light into the pervasive darkness of
the great riddle. He knows that there is a meaning in nature, that
the world conceals a mystery which it is the purpose of his life to
discover.

195   After Plato's problem—the eternal ideas—had fallen, like Sleep-
ing Beauty, into a sleep that lasted two thousand years, philosophy,

[19] In the novel *Lucas Heland* (Freiburg i. Br. and Berlin, 1897), by Ernst Kilchren,
pseudonym of Carl Albrecht Bernoulli (1868-1937), theologian and professor of
Church history at Basel University.
[20] Friedrich Schiller, *Die Horen* (1795), v. 134.
[21] Greek *panta rhei*, "all things flow," an interpretation of frag. 12 of the *Cosmic
Fragments* of Heraclitus, in which he states that "upon those who step into the same
river, different and again different waters flow," and of Plutarch's statement that
Heraclitus said that it was impossible to step into the same river twice. Cf. Heraclitus,
The Cosmic Fragments (Cambridge, England, 1954), p. 367.

in its manifold transmutations, prepared the way for the coming of the philosopher of Königsberg, who with a bold flourish awakened the ancient problem from its deathlike slumber and introduced it, dressed in new garb, to an awestruck world. What Kant did was to raise the question of the *Ding an sich*.

196　　The *Ding an sich* includes everything that eludes our perception, everything of which we have no tangible mental image. For example, for us the term "Rimatara" represents *Ding an sich*. Very likely none of us knows what Rimatara is. But looking in an atlas, we find that Rimatara is a South Sea coral atoll.[22] At once the *Ding an sich* turns into a tangible image. We picture an island possessing all those attributes that experience has taught us to ascribe to a South Sea isle. Thus we have a more or less graphic notion of Rimatara, i.e., we have turned the unknown into the known, we have diminished by one term the transcendental domain of the *Ding an sich*. Science does this across the board, expanding our mental universe by diminishing the realm of the unknown and intangible. It achieves this either by making positive discoveries, or by explaining phenomena. If we do not yet possess a graphic image of the cause of a phenomenon, we create a so-called principle, i.e., we postulate the existence of a *Ding an sich* that cannot be explained with the means now at our disposal. Thus it is easy to understand that in the past scientists formulated many principles which are no longer regarded as principles because of subsequent advances made in our knowledge of causal relations. For example, in the past there was a great deal of talk about the humid principle, the hot, the cold, the aqueous, and so on. Today we have recognized the source of these supposed principles, i.e., we have explained them through our discovery of higher chains of cause and effect. But once we have recognized the causes of a principle, it ceases to be a principle, for the *principium* is the first and the ultimate.

197　　The principles of modern science mark the extreme limit of our knowledge of the ever-lengthening causal sequences. There is no cause that might prevent our admission of further information, i.e., our discovery, through improved methods, of higher chains of cause and effect. But those people who are already triumphantly proclaiming to the world that everything will be explained in the very near future would do well to ponder the following basic tenet

[22] In the Austral Islands, French Polynesia.

of epistemology: According to the principle of sufficient reason, the chain of cause and effect is infinite. To be sure, we can hope that by magnifying the powers of our senses through some means, we will make great strides in acquiring knowledge of basic principles,[23] but we must always keep in mind that no cause is a final cause but rather still represents the effect of a cause. Viewing things in this light we can conceive of the existence of an infinite number of worlds that relate to each other like *concentric* and *eccentric* circles. Naturally these worlds are entirely subjective and of such a nature that, strictly speaking, every subject (of cognition) has his own. But experience shows that the worlds of individuals of the same species are more or less congruent because of the uniformity of their sense organs. The amoeba has its own special world, the worm has its world; so does the mammal, and so does man. The relationship between these various worlds depends on the quality of the sense organs involved. In the cited cases, the world of the amoeba is, roughly speaking, contained in that of the worm; the worlds of both in that of the mammal; and all three in that of man. Every world corresponding to more highly differentiated sense organs is related to all other worlds corresponding to less highly differentiated sense organs, as the world of the *Ding an sich* relates to that of man. At bottom, i.e., in itself, everything that exists, even "the well-known horde that spreads within the familiar sphere," moves within one and the same world: that which is unfathomably existent beneath the governance of an unknown final cause. The absolute realm is not divided into two distinct realms, the *Ding an sich* on the one hand and the phenomenal world on the other. All is One. A separation exists only in relation to us, because our sense organs are capable of perceiving only specific areas of the world-as-absolute.

198   (Note for the author.) I am well aware that what I have developed here is a more or less novel view of the derivation of the *Ding an sich*. But it seems to me that this is the only accurate and truly universal interpretation of the epistemological problem. Contrary to the view of absolute subjectivism, I must assert that before their discovery X-rays represented a *Ding an sich* to the same degree as the objects of the postulates of pure reason—God, freedom, and immortality.

[23] *Deleted*: but we will never arrive at a positive *end*.

199   Although, in his positive philosophy, Kant admitted a predominance of noumena fundamental for the derivation, just elaborated, the Kantian critique of epistemology left the problem of the *Ding an sich* unsolved. The first of the post-Kantian philosophers to do an intelligent job of making this problem once again useful to philosophy was Schopenhauer. As we know, Schopenhauer interpreted the *Ding an sich* as a blind Will. Schopenhauer's intellectual heir, Eduard von Hartmann, took over this concept of the Will, but added the element of the transcendental idea and interpreted the *Ding an sich* as intrinsically unconscious willing and imagination. Hartmann and Schopenhauer are monists, i.e., they interpret the world as arising from *one* single substance, from *one* single final cause of uncertain nature. But both men are endowed with lucid, causally oriented minds, and are also men of feeling, and therefore are pessimists with a sharp eye for the inner strife of the human heart and a sharp ear for the discord in the overture to every human life. They understood the profound significance, for philosophy, of human suffering; they have not, like those optimists who revert to the crassest barbarism and animality, arrogantly looked away from the unutterable pain suffered by all creatures. As every genuine philosopher must, they have assigned to suffering the chief place in their thought. Suffering is the first element that Schopenhauer derives from the blindness of his primal Will. Hartmann regards it as the ground of all existence. Even before Kant, dualism in philosophy was taboo, and thus Hartmann and Schopenhauer are also monists. But their hearts, their humane feelings, rebelled, and so they are forced to assign suffering a transcendental ground in the *Ding an sich*. Thus Schopenhauer's Will is blind because it has created a world full of suffering. And Hartmann's unconscious is not itself conscious and yet is and always has been unhappy, because it intentionally devised the best life possible, a life that is relatively happy compared to eternal wretchedness. On the other hand, if we take dualism as a basis—thereby failing to satisfy our striving for unity—we immediately possess an eminently sufficient reason for the suffering of the world. If we were to declare empiricism the only possible foundation of all speculative inquiry, then the dualistic world view would not seem so far off the mark.

200   Recent scientific research supplies us with some extremely valuable data on the subject of dualism. But before we move on to the moderns, it would be well to recall, in gratitude and appreci-

ation, the words of two men from the past who were widely separated in time and space.

201   Jesus Sirach says:[24]

> Opposite evil stands good,
>   opposite death, life;
>   so too, opposite the devout man stands the sinner.
> This is the way to view all the works of the Most High;
>   they go in pairs, by opposites.
>   —Ecclesiasticus 33:15-16[25]

202   Jakob Boehme[26] says: "Without opposition no thing can become
apparent to itself; for if there is nothing in it which resists it, it
goes forever outward and does not enter again into itself: But if it
does not enter again into itself, as into that whence it originally
went out, it knows nothing of its first condition."

203   At this point we must also recall Empedocles, who set up the
theory that multiplicity arises from enantiology, the opposition between the νεῖκος (strife) and φιλία (love) within the elements.

204   If we adopt a purely contemplative attitude toward nature, the
thought will impress itself upon us that somewhere in the depths
of nature there must be concealed something of unspeakable obtuseness, something that continually strives to suppress all independent activity and to paralyze every undertaking. This "something" may be the dull-witted, hidebound force that compels the
stone, when it is soaring along filled with a joyous sense of its own
power, to descend again out of the kingdom of the air; or the
envious zeal of the tall tree that seeks to deprive its weaker companions of the all-nourishing sunlight; or the disease that, with
tenacious endurance, eats its way through generations of burgeon-
ing life, striving to destroy it; or the boundless stupidity of matter
that resists every impulse but that, once it has absorbed an impetus,
clings to it with an idiot perseverance.

205   If we contemplate nature with objectivity, are we not compelled
to think: Two radically different powers are here engaged in a

---

[24] Jesus Sirach, generally known as Ben Sira, is traditionally identified as the author
of the Book of Ecclesiasticus (O.T. Apocrypha).
[25] Quoted here from *The Jerusalem Bible* (Roman Catholic).
[26] Jakob Böhme (1575-1624), German mystic and philosopher, whose system rested
on the thesis of the dualism of God and the necessity of evil. Jung cited Böhme
copiously in the writings of his late years.

furious struggle for domination? One power always laboring to level everything to the ground, smooth it out, even it, reduce it to quiet, suppress all activity and all motion, destroy all beauty, render everything peaceful, still, and dead? And the other forever laboring to confer life and color on everything, impart movement in all directions, liberate matter from the crushing embrace of matter, create a measureless profusion of shapes and forms?

206   So striking is the impression of antagonistic aims in nature, that this strife was even admitted into science in the form of a biological principle: the struggle for existence.

207   We are primarily dependent on the resources of general physics if we wish to investigate the sources of this antagonism. General physics, which must be understood to include physiology, undertakes to reduce all natural phenomena to certain principles, i.e., subjective final causes whose nature, for the time being, is still unknown. Thus we expect that in this science we will be able to discover all those primary forces that furnish a sufficient explanation of the antagonism in question.

208   For now let us confine ourselves to inorganic nature. The principles of all inorganic phenomena are gravitation, cohesion, adhesion, capillarity, absorption, elasticity, affinity, inertia, magnetism, electricity, heat, light, and motion. Today all these forces still have the status of principles; for the fact, for example, that we explain light in terms of motions of waves in ether has no particular meaning until it is possible to obtain a graphic mental image of the ether. If we look at this group of principles, it strikes us at once that they fall into two separate, more or less well-defined classes. First, there are those a priori principles inherent in matter; second, there are those that come in contact with matter only a posteriori. Among the first group are, definitely, light, heat, electricity, and motion; and conditionally, magnetism. To briefly characterize the first group: As absolute, primary forces they do not come under the law of the conservation of energy, for they do not represent transmutations of energy but are only the condition, the reason why tension and the relaxation of tension become possible and manifest. Thus they bear a negative relation to the second group. Only affinity occupies a remarkable median position. What they have in common is an element of attraction which, extensively, is observable particularly in gravitation, cohesion, adhesion, capillarity, and absorption, and intensively in affinity and inertia. The essence of all attraction is

the striving to place every point of matter, to the maximum extent possible, in a state of rest, and to maintain it in a constant state. Thus the characteristic of this group is the tendency toward passivity.

209   Now let us characterize the second group: The energy forms of light, heat, electricity, electromagnetism, and motion exert their effects through the law of the conservation of energy. The forces in this group are not, a priori, inherent in matter, for a body is not *eo ipso* hot or luminous or electric, etc., in the way that it is *eo ipso* inert or possesses the property of gravitation. The forces in this group can operate only with the assistance of the forces in the first group. Thus, for example, motion takes place only if a body is inert. Potential can turn to kinetic energy only in the presence of gravitational attraction, and a chemical discharge only in the presence of affinity. If the forces of the second group are made to operate on those of the first, we find that inertia is overcome by the impulse to motion, and if not, that this impulse returns to its source in the form of heat. Heat overcomes cohesion, and electricity chemical affinity. Some of the forces in both groups enter into a remarkable relationship of mutual dependency—heat and affinity, for example. Affinity almost certainly ceases to exist at a temperature of absolute zero, $-273°C.$ [$-469°F.$].

210   Magnetism occupies a median position between the two groups which can be explained in much the same way as the median role of affinity: namely by a relationship of mutual dependency which may exist between electromagnetism and inertia. As for elasticity, I must, to be honest, admit that up to now I have not yet succeeded in deriving it to my satisfaction. Perhaps it should be regarded as an inverse inertia, in that it represents the positive rejection of an impulse, whereas inertia constitutes a negative rejection.

211   The element common to this group may be described as a striving toward the extensive and intensive change of position, in other words a striving for unceasing activity. It would be useful here to recall the physical theory concerning these forces. Light, heat, and electricity are explained in terms of ether waves. One absolutely essential property of the ether is unlimited repulsion, i.e., the striving toward unlimited possibilities of change of position. Eduard von Hartmann establishes the same point, saying that there are two types of energetic elements, one group of which perpetually repel each other while the others exert a perpetual attraction. Thus we

have arrived at essentially the same result as Hartmann, with the difference that we took perception as our starting point, whereas Hartmann proceeded on the basis of theory. Zöllner, too, in his deliberations on the properties of matter, arrives at the admission of antagonistic tendencies, the simultaneous existence of attractive and repulsive forces. In other words, he arrives at a dualism founded deep within the dynamic properties of nature.

212   Kant proceeds along the same lines in his *Allgemeine Naturgeschichte und Theorie des Himmels*: "I have employed no forces other than those of attraction and repulsion to elaborate the great order of nature, two forces which are both equally *certain*, equally simple, and, at the same time, equally *primary* and *universal*."[27]

213   To summarize briefly what we have said so far concerning physical principles:

214   The essential element of gravitation, cohesion, adhesion, capillarity, absorption, inertia, affinity, and elasticity, is the positive striving to achieve absolute rest or neutrality.

215   The essential element of motion, light, heat, and electricity, is the positive striving toward unlimited change, eternal activity. The expression of their never-ending activity is the law of the conservation of energy.

216   Picture a world that has not yet been endowed with the active forces. Such a world would necessarily hang in the darkness of space "in an ugly lump," quiet, rigid, and dead, absolutely motionless and unchanging. Who, confronted with such a picture, would not recall the words of Moses: "And the earth was without form, and void; and darkness was upon the face of the deep" (Gen. 1:2). How could the earth have conceived life if it was not fitted out as a bride by the forces of activity?

217   "And God said, Let there be light"[28] (Gen. 1:3). When a creative act illuminated the dark chaos, the redemption of the world began, even before any organic being experienced the kindness of the all-merciful light.[29] The active force of heat first had to release the

[27] Kant, *Allgemeine Naturgeschichte und Theorie des Himmels, ein Versuch von der Verfassung und dem mechanischen Ursprunge des ganzen Weltgebäudes nach Newtonischen Grundsätzen abgehandelt* (Königsberg and Leipzig, 1755), introduction (n. p.). (Tr.: *Kant's Cosmogony in His Essay on the Retardation of the Rotation of the Earth and the Natural History and Theory of the Heavens*, Glasgow, 1900.)
[28] *Deleted*: and there was light.
[29] *Deleted*: When for the first time the sun flooded the dark earth with light.

elements from the solid aggregation of matter, had to separate the liquid from the solid and the gaseous from the liquid. It had to deliver matter from an unspeakable pressure, and once that had occurred, matter began to move. The liquid emerged and streamed over the surface of the planets. The gases boiled and seethed out of the rocks and the molten elements. The ardor of elective affinity began to emerge. The elements began to love and hate each other, and multiplicity was born out of their opposition.

218   Do we not see here an antagonism in the most primitive but also most prodigious form? Here are the roots of dualism. Here we are at the source. Here in inorganic nature are those forces of opposition that seek to overwhelm one another. Here is the place where that struggle begins that the philosophers term the suffering of the world. This primal and fundamental opposition between living and dead, active and passive, is the mighty minor chord with which the song of the world begins. It is this antagonism, which out of two conflicting elements composes the third, and the fourth, and the tenth, and the hundredth and thousandth.

219   "Thus we see," says Hartmann, "the divergence into a polarized dualism as the principle which generates the material world."

220   If we wish to avoid falling prey to idle fancies, we must regard this organic antagonism as the real, empirical basis of all speculation on the nature of the world. Wundt expresses this dualism in a genuinely classical form in his first two axioms of physics: "1) All causes in nature are causes of motion. 2) Every cause of motion exists outside that which is moved." Thus Wundt, too, feels compelled to admit, as the first principle of all formation in the world, a static factor and a factor inducing motion, both of which exist a priori.

221   Nor can Schelling avoid the principle of dualism on which all nature is grounded. Thus he says: "But if the absolute is to be evident to itself, it must, in accordance with its objective, appear dependent on something else, something alien to itself."

222   And what do we hear from the much-despised Jakob Boehme? "No thing can become apparent to itself without opposition."

223   Now that we have demonstrated the roots of dualism in the principles of physics, it remains to demonstrate dualism in the realm of organic nature. We can state a priori, with apodictic certainty, that we will encounter in the physical organism the same dualism that we have just demonstrated in inorganic matter. This

is easy to understand, in that the physical organism is the product of X interacting with the material forces of inorganic nature. The fundamental schism in material nature is, we will find, the precondition for the occurrence in the physical organism of the strange phenomenon of human suffering. Life undoubtedly represents the manifestation of the highest activity. The organism retains its own passionate urges despite the raging onslaught of all the laws of nature. For years on end it overcomes all resistance, overcomes all the obstacles presented by the laws of matter: gravitation, inertia, affinity, and so on. Hartmann says: "The entire life of a plant, as of an animal, constitutes an infinite sum of infinitely many acts of natural healing, for at every moment the onslaught of destructive physical and chemical influences must be paralyzed and overcome." The living organism is, quite simply, a miracle, in that it lifts itself above all those laws of physics that approach absolute reliability. Obviously the organism also satisfies physical laws, for after all, it is composed of matter. But this fact in no way constitutes a sufficient reason to deny the existence of a vital principle. To regard life merely as a complex physical structure is a sign of great confusion. The organism is involved in a never-ending struggle with the environment; this is the ultimate dualism of the organic phenomenon. Darwin perceived the nature of this dualism and conferred on it the dignity of a biological principle, to whose operations, to a large extent, he reduces the phenomenon of differentiation. In every self-conscious being, dualism appears in a dual form. Every conscious being has an external and an internal image of itself. In his text on physiological chemistry, Runge[30] goes into some detail concerning this idea of Schopenhauer. Our picture of dualism will be dual in accordance with the dual nature of perception. First we have the image of the external struggle for survival, and second we have the internal reflection of this struggle, in the form of a feeling of psychical schism:

> Alas, there dwell two souls in my breast,
> each desiring to part from the other.
> One, in the robust pleasure of love,
> clings to the earth with all its might.

[30] Friedlieb Ferdinand Runge (1795-1867), German chemist and professor at Breslau, whose notable discoveries include caffeine and atropine.

1. The closing lines of Jung's inaugural address, upon assuming the chairmanship of the Basel section (see p. 56)

2. Jung in his Zofingia Club regalia, about 1896

3. Members of the Basel section of the Zofingiaverein.
Jung is seated, third from left

4. The Basel pub called "Breo," the meeting-place of the Zofingia Society;
early 1890s

5. The final seven paragraphs of Lecture ɪᴠ, "Thoughts on the Nature and
Value of Speculative Inquiry" (see pp. 87-88)

The other prodigiously heaves itself from the dust
to enter the domain of noble forebears.[31]

224   Man's inner dualism is the direct continuation of the dualism of inorganic nature. Life is the highest activity we know, and thus everything that is less active will attempt to block its way. The entire external environment may act as an obstacle to the degree that it hinders the untrammeled operation of the organism. Every relationship to the environment represents an obstacle in that our environment is material and strives to attain the maximum possible degree of rest. Every relationship to the inner world, insofar as it is directed toward maximum activity, is supportive in that all activity unfolds more freely the further removed it becomes from any obstructive passivity. The causal instinct leads us, a priori, away from all externality to the inwardness of transcendental causes. Thus it continually directs us away from passivity and toward activity, as to our proper and primary nature, which has not, and ought not to have, anything in common with the obtuseness and inertia of material substance.

225   It is from the dualism grounded in the depths of nature that we derive justification for giving precedence, above all the other instincts, to the causal instinct, for this instinct alone points to the true root of our nature: unconditional activity. The pure contemplation of nature supplies us with unconditional affirmation of the causal instinct. Here we also have the objective reason for the subjective appearance of the source of greatest happiness, which is attained through gratification of the need for causality. No man feels well and happy until he finds others of his own kind. The closer we approach to the roots of our own being, the more unalloyed and the more enduring our happiness becomes.

226   Now that we have demonstrated the teleological element in the category of causality and the universal ethical justification of speculative inquiry, it remains for us to briefly depict the results of the affirmation of the causal instinct.

227   One of the first results will be to reject the secularization of human interests, i.e., the focal point of all concern will shift from the material to the transcendental world as a result of the perception that, with respect to the determination of our human nature,

---

[31] Goethe, *Faust I*, "Outside the City Gate."

the relation to material things is not purposeful. We will reject the will to material existence as inexpedient for the development of the activity inherent to our nature. On the other hand we will affirm the will to personality, to individuality, in the sense of the most radical diversity between an individual and everything else that exists, as the most radical diversification is consistent with the activity inherent to our nature, and thus the will to diversity is purposeful. The justification of suicide as the most certain and most complete expression of the negation of the Will—a justification that Schopenhauer attempts to disprove in an intricate sophism—must be rejected on the basis of the elementary perception that no diversity can develop without the existence of an opposite, and thus that the suffering resulting from dualism is absolutely essential to the development of a differentiated personality.

228   The basic tenor of the dualistic world-view, immanent pessimism, is determined by the painful but true perception that for the most part our actions and those of our fellow men are unpurposeful with respect to the metaphysical purpose of man, and that, as regards the present state of the phenomenal world, life, as Schopenhauer says, is nothing but suffering.[32]

229   Every genuine philosophy, every true religion is wrapped in the earthly garment of pessimism as the only accurate mode of reviewing the world befitting man in the awareness of his nothingness. The fact that certain men, who are otherwise of good reputation, make a great point of claiming that they are optimists, and disparage all pessimism as unhealthy, even forgetting themselves so far as to make Lord Byron's clubfoot responsible for his pessimism, and to attribute Schopenhauer's pessimism to a case of syphilis contracted in Venice, is the result of their failure to reflect on the true nature of optimism, and their failure to have ever poked their noses into Schopenhauer's works. In Schopenhauer they would have found passages like the following: "If one could lead the hardened optimist through the civilian and military hospitals, the surgical horror-houses, through the prisons, torture chambers, and slave barracks, across the battlefields and past the places of execution; then open to him all the gloomy habitations where misery creeps away to hide from cold glances of curiosity; and finally let

[32] Schopenhauer, *Die Welt als Wille und Vorstellung*, Vol. I, § 56.

230   him peer into Ugolino's starvation chamber;[33] surely in the end he too would perceive the nature of this *meilleur des mondes possibles.*"[34]

At another point he writes: "I cannot refrain from stating that optimism, insofar as it is not merely the thoughtless chatter of those whose trivial heads house nothing but words, appears to me not merely an absurd but a genuinely impious way of thinking, a bitter contempt for the nameless sufferings of mankind."[35]

231   Thus Schopenhauer neatly disposes of the optimists. The optimist's *joie de vivre* has always been viewed as inseparable from a measure of stupidity, as we see from the following passage of Aristotle: ... πάντες ὅσοι περιττοὶ γεγόνασιν ἄνδρες ἢ κατὰ φιλοσοφίαν ἢ πολιτικὴν ἢ ποίησιν ἢ τέχνας φάνονται μελαγχολικοὶ ὄντες (... all those who have become eminent in philosophy or politics or poetry or the arts are clearly of melancholy temperament).[36]

232   Today it seems to me of the greatest importance that we remind ourselves, in all humility, that there is such a thing as reason, and a religion called Christianity which some of us proudly claim to embrace, and that both categorically point us in the direction of pessimism. Recently people appear to have forgotten this, and no longer wish to recall that every transcendental world-view is pessimistic. They have banished metaphysics and, with boundless idiocy, make a lot of pretty speeches about ethics free of metaphysics, which naturally results in the crassest optimism. There are even Christian theologians who are optimists and who presumably do not know that "the whole cosmos is grounded in evil" (ὅτι ὁ κόσμος ὅλος ἐν τῷ πονηρῷ κεῖται). Well, each to his own pleasure.

233   If we glance back at our rather lengthy chain of reasoning about the nature and value of speculative inquiry, we find that we seem to have covered pretty much everything that could be covered within the framework of a brief lecture.

234   In conclusion I would like to express the hope that at least a little of what I have said will stick with you, and that the extraordinarily

---

33 Ugolino della Gherardesca (d. 1209), a Ghibelline who connived with the enemy party, the Guelphs, and was eventually imprisoned by the Ghibellines he had betrayed, along with his three sons and two grandsons, in a tower where they starved to death. Dante describes the fate of this traitor in *Inferno*, canto 33.

34 *Die Welt als Wille und Vorstellung*, Vol. I, § 59.

35 Ibid.

36 Aristotle, *Problems*, Book XXX, 953 a, in *The Complete Works*, revised by Jonathan Barnes (Bollingen Series LXXI:2, 1983), here modified.

intriguing problem of a priori causality has not been introduced in vain.

235   Finally, I would like to quote a fine passage from Nietzsche: "I say to you, one must yet have chaos in himself in order to give birth to a dancing star."

236   A better alternative: "He who in everything seeks to detect the untruth and who voluntarily keeps company with misery, may find that a different miracle of disillusionment is being prepared for him. Something unutterable, of which happiness and truth are no more than graven idols, is making its way toward him. The earth is losing its gravity, the events and powers of the earth are turning into dreams, and a transfiguration as of summer evenings envelops him. He who beholds this feels as if he were just beginning to wake up, and as if all that remains of the world around him is no more than the vanishing clouds of a dream. In time these too will blow away: for the day has come."

V

THOUGHTS ON THE INTERPRETATION OF CHRISTIANITY, WITH REFERENCE TO THE THEORY OF ALBRECHT RITSCHL

(January 1899)

PRAEFATIO
AUDITORI BENEVOLO![1]

237   People have every right to feel surprised to see a medical student abandon his craft during his clinical training to speak about theological issues. Several considerations might dissuade me from taking this step. I know that I am not going to earn any laurels, but that instead I am running the risk of being sent back to my own little nook with an indignant "Cobbler, stick to your last!"

238   I know that my acquaintance with theological matters is far too sketchy to permit reliable judgments based on a broad knowledge of the field. I know that theologians will find it easy to accuse me of being overhasty in some of my inferences and judgments. They live amid the ideas and concepts of their science, and they will be as swift to detect the imperfect outfit of the intruder, as a medical man would be to note the inevitable flaws displayed by a usurper in the realm of physical science. If any professional theologians are interested in finding out how insecure I feel, I extend to them a friendly invitation to come over (to the medical school) and try their luck on our ground.

239   However, I am determined to take this step into the unknown because of the error that I hate and fear as much as I do living a worthless life. What I want is to dispel error and to create clarity both for myself and for others. Thus I am also moved by *justice*, by the desire to refrain from doing anyone an injustice, and simply to listen and investigate before I form any judgment.

240   But the final and highest cause for my decision to abandon the solid ground under my feet is truth. That truth that since the beginning of time has lain within the shining eyes of the child, with their unheeding, pensive, faraway look; in life with its wild craving and ardent fire, this wretched life beneath the revolving heaven full of transitory stars; and in the staring eye of the dying with their unheeding, pensive, faraway look.

[1] "Preface for my gracious audience!"

91

241   The truth compels me to desert my plow before the noontide, to abandon my labor in the fields of my chosen profession, and to ask that we all raise our eyes from our work and look toward the west where the sun, in accordance with ancient custom, will end the day which we have called by name.

242   As an ignorant amateur I hesitate to enter the sanctum sanctorum of an unfamiliar science, and risk being somewhat roughly shown the door again. And yet as a human being I expect hospitality even from adversaries.

THOUGHTS ON THE
INTERPRETATION OF CHRISTIANITY,
WITH REFERENCE TO THE THEORY
OF ALBRECHT RITSCHL[2]

A single spark of the fire of justice, fallen into the soul of a learned man, is enough to irradiate, purify, and consume his life and endeavors, so that he no longer has any peace and is forced to abandon forever that tepid or cold frame of mind in which run-of-the-mill savants carry out their daily chores.

—Nietzsche

243   If we cast a glance down the long procession of the centuries, we find scattered, like so many points of light, throughout the history of the development and the vicissitudes of worldly powers, strange figures who appear to belong to a different order: alien, almost supramundane beings who relate to the historical conditions just enough to be understood, but who essentially represent a new species of man. The world does not give birth to them, but rather they create a world, a new heaven and a new earth. Their values are different, their truths are new. They know that they are necessary and that we have been waiting for them, that we have awaited them a long time, and that it is for them alone that causal sequence of the world's historical development has plowed the fields and prepared them to receive the seed, or ripened the grain for harvest. They come into the world as if it belonged to them and see themselves as the incarnation of a purpose for which an infinite number of deeds has prepared the way. They know that they are the meaning and the end toward which the labor of many centuries has been directed, and that now they have become the material representation of this end. They identify with the idea they bring to the world, and they live out this idea feeling that it will endure forever and that it is beyond violation by the exegesis of men. They *are* their own idea, untrammeled and absolute among the minds of

[2] For Jung's textual notes for this lecture, see the appendix.

93

their age, and not susceptible to historical analysis, for they experience the products of history not as conditions of their being but rather as the object of their activity, and as their link with the world. They have not evolved from any historical foundation, but know that in their inmost natures they are free of all contingency, and have come only in order to erect on the foundation of history the edifice of their own ideas.

244 One such man was Jesus of Nazareth. He knew this and he did not hesitate to proclaim it to the world.

245 Human beings have never possessed yardsticks with which to measure great minds. For centuries they have debated whether Christ was a god, a god-man, or a man. The Middle Ages assumed the absolute reliability of all the New Testament accounts concerning the person of Christ. The Middle Ages lacked the yardstick by which to measure Christ. A god is *qualitas occulta*; a god-man even more so; and man is absolutely incommensurable with Christ. Thus Christ was a god-man or God, a quality that cannot be further elucidated.

246 The situation has changed radically during the evolution of modern, post-Renaissance philosophy. Over the years epistemology, which constitutes the fundamental problem of all philosophy, has gradually developed a concept essential for general mental operations, namely the concept of the normal man. To be sure, the normal man is not a quantity acknowledged by public statute, but rather is a product of tacit convention, a thing that exists everywhere and nowhere, to which all epistemological results refer implicitly. Just as a Paris cellar now harbors a standard meter by which all other instruments of measurement are calibrated, so, in an indetectable place inside the heads of scientific-minded men, there exists the standard of the normal man that is used to calibrate all scientific-philosophical results.

247 Modern people no longer acknowledge the New Testament accounts to be absolutely reliable, but only relatively reliable. Armed with this judgment, critical scholarship lays hold of the person of Christ, snips a bit off here and another bit off there, and begins—sometimes covertly and sometimes overtly, blatantly, and with a brutal naïveté—to measure him by the standard of the normal man. After he has been distilled through all the artful and capricious mechanisms of the critics' laboratory, the figure of the historical Jesus emerges at the other end. The man with the scientist's retort in his hand is no longer interested in this body which has now been

made to conform to the standard of the normal man and patented for international consumption, and leaves it up to the world to decide whether it wishes to welcome this Christ as God, as a god-man, or as a man.

248 The Germanic variety of the species *Homo sapiens* has a reputation for particular sensibility and depth of feeling. This may be true of the German nation as a whole, but great scholars whose achievements are acknowledged in their lifetimes constitute an exception. It is really astounding how little emotion a truth, a piece of scientific knowledge, actually does arouse in our men of learning. How could Kant, who regarded God as a *Ding an sich*, as a "purely negative limiting concept," still have any religion; and how could he himself, as an unknowable *Ding an sich*, exist in the cheerless desert of this "negative limiting concept"? How can Wundt wax enthusiastic over the ethical purpose of the world, when nothing exists that could achieve or enjoy this purpose? How can Hartmann attribute any kind of impulse for ethical action to the void and unfeeling unconscious? And finally, how can Albrecht Ritschl[3] be a committed Christian, when his God is compelled to go through official channels whenever he wishes to do something good for man?

249 An incredible want of sensibility is required to arrive at conclusions like these, and not to feel pierced to the heart. Probably the savants to whom I have alluded suffer from overwork and have no time to experience personally the heights and depths of emotion which must properly attend their views, or to live them out in fear and trembling. A man who fails to live out his own truth will fail to detect its results. And yet it is only by knowing the results of a truth that we become aware of its internal contradictions. As a rule, one does not need to look far to detect some absurdity, some caprice or logical flaw in their ideas.

250 If we wish to make sense of Ritschl's Christianity, we must always keep in mind this want of sensibility which typically characterizes men acknowledged as notable scholars.[4]

251 Indisputably Ritschl's is the most significant and original of all

[3] Albrecht Ritschl (1822-1889), German Protestant theologian, who denied the mystical element in religion; author of *Die Christliche Lehre von der Rechtfertigung und Versöhnung* (1870-1874) (The Christian doctrine of justification and atonement).
[4] *Originally*: This want of feeling so typical for prominent scholars is the most generous excuse that can be offered for the aberration of modern theology, which Ritschl initiated in a pseudoliterature amalgamated out of Kantian and Lutheran ideas.

modern interpretations of Christ and his teachings. I must confess that I was genuinely amazed to encounter so much of solid philosophical value during my study of Ritschl's writings. If we take the theologians at their word, we might expect to find nothing in Ritschl but what theologians term "the simple preachment of the human personality of Christ." But Ritschl's theories are in no way simple or easily accessible. Instead they constitute an extremely artful epistemology which, in genuine Kantian fashion, is calibrated wholly with reference to the normal man; a keen-witted, compelling line of reasoning; a profound intimacy with the philosophical problem of Illuminism; and all in all a first-rate, logical, and extremely conclusive development of Kantian epistemology based on a solid foundation of Lutheranism. All things which our theologians have always taken pains to conceal. For example, quite recently theorists who hold the historical view of Christianity did not say boo when Vischer,[5] in his study, spoke about illuministic knowledge, but instead applauded as if such knowledge were completely compatible with the historical view. I have been listening attentively to theologians for more than two years now, vainly hoping to gain a clue to their mysterious concept of human personality. Vainly I sought to discover where human personality gets its motivational force. Apparently the depiction of his human personality is intended to present us with a clearly-defined image. The formation of an ethical character should result from the holding up of the image, either through some secret correspondence inaccessible to perception or, more naturally, this image is supposed to serve as a model to awaken in us the impulse to imitate Christ. The Ancients were already employing this second method centuries ago, when Theseus or Solon was held up as a model to an Athenian youth. The image of the Buddha is drummed into the Hindu boy, or a holy fakir is paraded before him. A boy who reads *Robinson Crusoe* becomes so enthusiastic about the protagonist that his actions are determined by those of his hero, in accordance with that same law of nature that decrees that a black man cannot refrain from wearing the top hat and studs of the European. If one simply chose to yield to every impulse to mimicry, one could, just for the fun of it, go around with one's head bowed in deep thought, allowing oneself to be possessed by the personality of Hegel, and end up bewitching the

[5] F. T. von Vischer, author of *Auch Einer* (1884).

world with theories about absolute, a priori Being In-and-Of-Itself, Through-Itself, and For-Itself. We can find as much motivation in any other personality—and even more in those modern personalities with whom we are more familiar—than in the personality of Christ, who is so widely separated from us both in time and through the interpretations. What then is so special about Christ, that he should be the motivational force?[6] Why not another model—Paul or Buddha or Confucius or Zoroaster? The compelling character of moral values derives from metaphysics alone, for as Hartmann says, ethics divorced from metaphysics has no ground to stand on. If we view Christ as a human being, then it makes absolutely no sense to regard him as, in any way, a compelling model for our actions. Under these circumstances it will be a hopeless undertaking to try to convince the world of the necessity of Christian ethics. But if, as Ritschl does, we presuppose the dogma of Christ's divinity, the problem ceases to be that of why Christian ethics is valid in the first place, and is reduced to the more limited problem of the *mode* of determination of ethical action.

252   I will now move on to describe Ritschl's theory of the compelling character of the personality of Christ for Christian moral action.

253   Everything real, that is, every object of cognition, arouses a sensation. It is the function of memory to store up such sensations. At any time memory can reproduce for us the image of an event that originally was real. The image in memory consists of two distinct objects. The first is the image of the original event, and the second is the image of the feeling aroused in us by the original event. Thus the first part of memory contains only the image of the *actus purus*, the pure event, but the second tells us what kind of feeling—pleasure or aversion—the event awakened in us. From this second part of the image in memory arises the idea and the feeling of value that we ascribe to the event, which being pure is, as such, neutral. Thus the image in memory consists of our idea of the pure event, combined with the sense of value. In accordance

---

[6] *Deleted*: A theologian really has neither the right nor the power to prevent anyone from taking it into his head to imitate Napoleon or Kaiser Wilhelm. So, when the theologians could not or did not wish to enlighten me, I went to the model on my own, and now I will tell and reveal to you with dispassion what arguments Ritschl presents to justify his doctrine, and what, for unfathomable reasons, the theologians conceal from themselves.

with the dictum *Nihil est in intellectu, quod non antea fuerit in sensu,*[7] we are accustomed to trace every feeling we experience to an external stimulus. Thus it can easily happen that we relate a feeling to an external, material event, and equate this feeling with a genuine sensation. In most cases this relation will actually exist, but in some it may not. Probably we are particularly susceptible to such error in matters of religion. I will clarify this with a concrete example.

254 In the time of Christ there was a legend that at certain moments an angel would stir the waters of the pool at Bethesda. Let us suppose that at one time an angel really did stir the water and that someone witnessed this event. This person passed on to others the image of the event as he remembered it. At this point the image in his memory passes into the heads of his audience, and they link this image with the feeling of value that people customarily ascribe to the appearance of an angel. Now the water bubbles up again, in the same way as the image in their memory, and inevitably they associate with the event the sense of value imparted to them by the man who originally told the tale. But being endowed with lively imaginations, they confuse what is merely a subjective feeling with a sensation produced by a material stimulus. But every sensation derives from an actual event external to ourselves, to which we refer the sensation. For this reason people believe that an angel has actually stirred up the water and produced this sensation—or rather this feeling—in them by his presence. Thus the emotion-based hallucination of an angel stems from an unconscious confusion of a feeling felt in the past, which is now merely remembered, with a truly existent feeling produced by objective causes.

255 This is the way Ritschl analyzes objects of a religious nature, above all the problem of the *unio mystica,* the direct relationship of a human being to God and Christ which is claimed by many so-called "pietists."

256 The Gospel-writers transmit to us the image of what they remember about Christ. As we have said, what is communicated is merely the pure, undifferentiated image, but the image is closely linked with the sense of value that has been instilled in the human race. If a man now performs a Christian act consistent with the

7 "Nothing exists in the intellect that did not previously exist in the senses" (Aristotle via the Scholastics).

Christ he remembers, the feeling of value originally transmitted to and instilled in him by the Evangelists, which he recalls in the moment his Christian motivation is realized in action, deceives him into believing that he is experiencing a genuine sensation, and he falls prey to the notion that this sensation results from some objective cause external to himself, namely the actual and effectual presence of Christ. That is, he believes that Christ himself, in an objective and material form, is standing beside him and has entered into a real, tangible relationship with him. The same process explains the direct relationship that allegedly exists between a human being and God.

257   Thus Ritschl rejects any illuministic or subjective knowledge, and consequently also rejects the *unio mystica*, that object on which all medieval mysticism was focused and which, down to our civilized and enlightened times, has been pursuing its wicked ways inside the heads and hearts of otherwise irreproachable and right-thinking folk. But Ritschl does not maintain this negative attitude, but rather founds his ethics on the power of subjective feeling. He does this with such skill and bewildering dexterity that without incurring the slightest strain or misapprehension, it is possible for him to continue using the same vocabulary, with reference to the god-man relationship, that has hitherto been current in "pietistic" circles. Naturally this fact poses no small obstacle to a genuine and penetrating understanding of Ritschl's theory; this is why, for a non-theologian, the discourse of a dyed-in-the-wool Ritschlian seems to be a conglomeration of contradictions and ambiguities.[8] Of course no theologian will admit that this is the case. But I must say that the technical terms employed by the modern theologian are so abstruse and misleading that even educated people must engage in an abdication of the intellect in order to understand what is meant, on the symbolic or magical level, by a phrase like "religious-ethical motive." And when, finally, a Ritschlian construction is placed on an idea which continues to be addressed under the same old names, one can only gape in amazement and patiently endure the

---

[8] *Deleted*: To forestall confusion I will not, in what follows, give you literal quotations from Ritschl, for his syntax is distinguished by its great complexity and, often, its sheer incomprehensibility, at least for those who are merely hearing the words. A sentence which has to be read two or three times before one can understand it will not be comprehensible to someone who hears it read aloud just once.

incredible spectacle. At the end one will probably say to one's neigh
bor: "I suppose that's how it must be?!"

258   Ritschl's foundation of ethics derives from the same epistemo
logical basis as his refutation of Illuminism.

259   The so-called "pietist" says: "I stand in a direct and intimate
relationship to God. His nearness and the power of his presence
determine me to direct my actions in accordance with his will, i.e.
to act morally." On the aforementioned grounds Ritschl refutes
the unmediated nature of such a relationship, explaining the *unio
mystica* as resulting from the confusion of a subjective feeling of
value with an objectively determined sensation. Ritschl develops
his foundation of ethics entirely within the sphere of discursive
reason and sensory perceptibility. He states: "We cannot demonstrate that others can act on the human mind except within the
sphere of active and conscious sensation."

260   That is, one person can act on another only if the stimulus exerted
is received and processed within the other's sphere of consciousness. In fact it is impossible for any human consciousness to be
affected except within the sphere of sensory perceptibility, or rather
of "conscious sensation."

261   Thus, according to Ritschl, no effect can be exercised on a man's
consciousness except by way of conscious sensation. By this theory
the possibility, long ago established by science, of the existence of
so-called posthypnotic suggestion, is really an impossibility,[9] and so
on. Man draws the entire content of consciousness from the sphere
of conscious sensation, of sensory perceptibility. Thus he also acquires all motivation for ethical action by way of conscious sensation, in other words from the communications of other human
beings. The communication we receive from others is an image
drawn from memory. As we have already explained, this image
contains only the idea of the thing communicated and the feeling
of value we ascribe to the idea. Depending on the degree of value
we ascribe to an idea, it may become the motivation of our actions.
The subjective feeling of value confers on this idea, which in itself
is neutral and passive, the power of motivation, effectiveness, and
thus reality. So we lend being and reality to a mere passive idea.
We feel our "mental reality," but this reality is determined by a

9 *Deleted*: the same being true of premonitions, etc.

motivation whose only reality derives from the feeling of value we confer upon it. But the reality of the feeling of value has its ground in the reality of self-esteem. Ritschl formulates this rather complex thought in the following terms: "The dignity attached to our mental reality is the sufficient cognitive reason for the reality of everything that contributes to our reality, as a valuable and effective existence in the world."

262   We see, or rather we fail to see, that what we have here is a sort of tall tale in which someone pulls himself out of the swamp by his own topknot.

263   As a rule feelings of value respecting ethical actions are instilled in us by others. The inculcation of these feelings occurs through communication. The child is taught that Christ helped the poor and infirm. This is the *actus purus*, the image in memory that does not involve any power to motivate. The child confers this power on the act after he has been taught that it is good to help the poor. By this process the feeling of value ascribed to the action is intensified so that finally the idea of helping the poor becomes so effective, by virtue of the intensified feeling of value, that it serves to motivate a similar action. The motivation of every Christian action is supplied in this way. The Evangelists transmit to us their memory of the deeds of Christ. The feeling of value instilled in us toward ethical action fastens itself to the idea—neutral in itself— of the moral life of Christ, and confers on this idea that efficacy that it must possess in order to motivate our will. The deeper we penetrate into the historical personality of Christ, the more notions of moral action we adopt, and the more motivations we acquire for our will.

264   Ritschl sees no other way to acquire motivations with respect to value, than the way of conscious sensation, and thus he is entirely dependent on those images in memory, supplied us by the most ancient sources, concerning the life of Christ. Ritschl's theory of the relationship of man with God and Christ derives from this epistemological necessity.

265   Moreover, since Ritschl, too, has built in his mind a tabernacle dedicated to the fictive "normal man," he knows, for reasons already stated, that no man can be acted upon by another outside the sphere of "conscious sensation," and thus that no man has access to any other sources of motivation than are contained in the Holy Scriptures. In Ritschl's view the New Testament, in the final

sense, teaches us the life of Christ. Or quite simply, Christ produces his life in us. At this point the so-called "pietist" will fall into a trap and say: This is in fact the *unio mystica*. Far from it! True, the words sound extremely mystical, and St. Francis of Assisi could say them without blushing. We are tempted to cite a slightly amended verse from Goethe:

> One hears the Gospel, but *one* lacks the faith!
> Faith is the dearest child of miracle![10]

266   Ritschl says quietly: "God punishes me through repentance. Christ consoles and encourages me."

267   But keep in mind that this pious sentiment applied only to the extent that the Christ present to the Ritschlian Christian constitutes the sum of all the images in memory handed down by tradition, that is, of all mental images concerning the person of Christ, in conjunction with the feeling of value that we confer on the totality of the images. For the Ritschlian, God and Christ always exist only in a special sense. On the other hand, the "pietist" holds that Christ consoles him, actually and directly, through the power of the Holy Spirit which Christ once promised to send to his own people. But the enlightened Ritschlian, who has learned the lessons of modern civilization, knows that God or Christ is not really materially present (*in substantia*), but only insofar as man, by virtue of the feeling of value that has been instilled in him, confers on the intrinsically unreal mental idea the power of motivating his actions and the property of real existence.

268   In classical antiquity the demigod Prometheus sang happily while he worked:

> Here I sit creating human beings . . .[11]

269   The Ritschlian can claim, among other things:

> Here I sit creating gods!

270   It appears that modesty increases with the advance of civilization! Furthermore, this compromise which Ritschl effects between Luther and Kant has an ominous taint of Kantian subjectivism and—hard though it is to imagine it—of the World as Will and Idea! Oh,

[10] Goethe, *Faust I*, lines 262-263, from "Night, the Gothic Room."
[11] Goethe, "Prometheus."

if only Schopenhauer had had the pleasure of seeing his ideas turned to account in this way! Perhaps we might modestly suggest to Mr. von Falkenberg that in the next edition of his history of modern philosophy, he might—in addition to the "untimely" non-philosopher Nietzsche[12]—cite Albrecht Ritschl as a secret admirer of Schopenhauer.

271   Many of my audience who are not in the least averse to employing Ritschl's symbolic language[13] may perhaps be horrified to perceive the abyss of anti-Christian notions, underlying this language, which I have just revealed to them. Indeed, assuming that I may always have defended myself with might and main against Ritschl's ideas, they may imagine that I have exaggerated a bit. But in fact I can quote from Ritschl word-for-word passages demonstrating that his brand of Christianity is actually as I have described it, and will do so now.

272   For example, Ritschl reproaches his adversaries who follow a concrete interpretation of Christ's promise: "And lo, I am with you always, even unto the end of the world,"[14] claiming that there exists a direct relationship, a *unio mystica*, between a man and God or Christ. Ritschl says of them: "They posit, as the reality of things, what are nothing more than unauthenticated and unstable images in memory."

273   On the other hand Ritschl knows that the only way to act upon a man's sphere of consciousness is through memory, whose power to motivate action is based on the subjective feeling of value. Thus he says: "However, a precise and detailed memory constitutes the form in which the human mind acquires all effectual and meritorious motivations, obedience to which enables us to live up to our proper purpose in life.

274   "For an exact memory is the medium of personal relationships, that is, it enables one person to exercise a continuous effect on another and to be present in him whenever the latter acts on the

[12] Jung is alluding to Nietzsche's *Unzeitgemässe Betrachtungen* (Untimely reflections), and to the fact that Nietzsche presented himself not as a philosopher intent on system-building in the traditional German manner but rather as a psychologist with a brilliant and aphoristic style which Nietzsche regarded as modeled on the French.
[13] *Deleted*: who are still gorging themselves on the feast which Ritschl has set before theology.
[14] Matt. 28:20. *Deleted*: or, "For where two or three are gathered together in my name, there am I in the midst of them" [Matt. 18:20].

basis of the former's teaching or instigation. And in the broadest sense this is true of the bond, in religion, between our lives and God, effected through our precise remembrance of Christ. However, we ought not to describe such relationships, and in particular the last-named relationship, as unmediated, for by doing so we declare them to be imaginary. For nothing is real that does not involve a large measure of mediation. But the personal relationship between God or Christ and ourselves is always mediated through our precise memory of the Word, that is, of the law and promise of God, and God acts on us only by means of one or the other of these revelations. The assertion, as a basic principle, of the unmediated nature of any perception or relationship, does away with the possibiltiy of distinguishing between reality and hallucination."

275   Then Ritschl recapitulates once more in order to forestall any possible misinterpretation. "Thus without the mediation of the Word of God, that is, the Law and the Gospel, and without the exact remembrance of this personal revelation of God in Christ, no personal relationship exists between a Christian and God."

276   I believe that this is clear and requires no further commentary. If the high priest who presided over the trial of Christ were not such an unsympathetic figure, one might indeed be tempted to exclaim as he did: "What further need have we of witnesses? behold, now ye have heard his blasphemy" [Matt. 26:65].

277   It remains for us to take a look at the world-view that emerges from Ritschl's epistemology. In the drama of the universe as perceived by Ritschl, God, Christ, and man play a truly pathetic role. A God who exists only to the degree, and can affect the order of the world only to the extent, that human beings ascribe to his image in their memory the power to motivate their actions. Christ is the same fumbling and helpless God turned into a man, and as a man is a wretched dreamer who suffers from hallucinations and moreover, as Ritschl aptly remarks, is "not very well-versed in the literature of mysticism"—a trait that he loyally shares with his epigone Paul. For Ritschl literally says: "Those who uphold their claim to a direct personal relationship with Christ or God are clearly not very well-versed in the literature of mysticism."

278   We may make light of Ritschl's God, but we can feel nothing but pity for Ritschl's Christian. Every pagan has his gods to whom he can cry out when he feels sorrowful and afraid, even if this god is

nothing but a brightly polished boot, a silver button, or a stick of wood. But Ritschl's Christian knows that his God exists only in church, school, and home and owes his efficacy to the subjectively determined power of motivation supplied by memory. And it is to this powerless God that a Christian is supposed to pray for salvation from bodily and spiritual want? God cannot lift a finger, for he exists only historically, in tradition, and in a strictly limited sense. The French could just as easily, and with just as little success, importune Charlemagne to inflict a great defeat on the wretched Germans and liberate Alsace-Lorraine.

279 At this point I will recall that want of feeling typical of notable scholars. This local demon that hops about in the desert of the heart has played a nasty trick on Ritschl.

280 Albrecht Ritschl is much more accessible when approached from a psychological point of view. He was a professor in Göttingen, a Lutheran institution, and was obliged to teach in accordance with Lutheran doctrine; thus he had to be a Lutheran. Ritschl's guideline was that famous blow by which Luther abruptly did away with all mysticism and the entire prophetic tradition of the ancient church. Ritschl himself states: "I am neither obligated nor entitled to teach in another way. Yet it is a noteworthy fact that a theologian like Weiss should dare to judge me by his pietistic pretensions, when I do not deviate from the teachings prescribed by Reformation doctrine."

281 Lutheranism was his absolute basis. In addition, as was proper for a respectable teacher of divinity, he was compelled to grapple with secular philosophy to a sufficient degree to show that Kantian epistemology was entirely compatible with Lutheran Christianity.

282 But the philosopher of Königsberg allows no one to play around with his ideas with impunity. The normal man in Kant's critique of pure reason has little taste for the element of mystery in religion, and seduced Ritschl to deny that mystery which slumbers in every human breast, so that he was swallowed up by that caste of men whose life and work consists in ignoring questions and stimulating certainty.

283 The prodigious history of mystery in the drama of the universe surges by, swallowing up the puny circles described by Ritschl. An intimation from infinity breathes over all human exegesis and blows it away. But the mystery will remain in the human heart until the end of time.

284   Clearly we have made little progress in understanding the person
of Christ. Quite apart from all the absurd interpretations and imputations made concerning Christ—sociopolitical aperçus, ideas
which satisfy the desire to "get a human slant on things," and so
on, which are cursed by their own absurdity from the moment of
their birth—it must still appear very strange to any educated layman
who is earnestly struggling to understand Christ, to see how he is
treated by theologians, the guardians and keepers of the highest
of earthly goods. In their naïveté theologians believe that the world
is so sweet and good that the only thing needed to get everyone
on earth to fling himself at the feet of this Model enthusiastically
is to preach a sermon about the person of Christ. They think that
the mere holding-up of the remembered image is sufficient to
determine moral action. Apparently many of our theologians are
so convinced of the goodness of the world that they believe everyone will immediately ascribe a feeling of value to this remembered
image, and so will confer on it the power to act in their hearts.
Obviously they do not know how utterly indifferent the world is
to sermonizing and preachers who throw up their hands in dismay.
The "purely . . . unstable image in memory" *cannot* stir the world
because no feeling of value with regard to the person of Christ has
yet been instilled in it. The world has not been taught about Christ
and has no interest in him. We still know far too little about how
Christ viewed himself, about his claim to divinity; and we still understand too little of Christ's concept of his own metaphysical significance to endow him with feelings of value. For the most part,
today's practical theologians have in fact abandoned the notion of
winning over the world through education and conviction. They
simply ignore the moral physiology espoused by their master Ritschl,
the second clause of which relates to the feeling of value, and
blithely preach away about the historical Jesus whose mere image
has no power to motivate. On the contrary, the repetition of this
theme every Sunday is turning it into a bore. To avoid the onerous
task of educating the human race to accept new points of view,
theologians prefer to just shrug their shoulders, say "Non liquet,"
and give in to a critical world. Indeed, they are willing to concede
three-quarters of the personality of Christ—his faith in miracles,
his prophetic powers, and his consciousness of his own divinity.
They confine themselves to preaching the historical Jesus, Christ
as a human being, a departure from Ritschl, but the reduction of

a high point to a lesser one. In the end Christ becomes a "naïve idealist," poor as a churchmouse, stripped of his power and glory and even his keen discernment. Naturally these experiments and concessions substantially reduce the chances of winning the world, and we are already seeing signs that eventually we will be driven to employ Salvation Army techniques, encumber religious services with all sorts of tricky devices, decorate churches inside and out with pretty frippery, install baptismal fonts and communion tables which rotate to the sound of music and come equipped with periodic changes of scenery, and set up, at appropriate spots, automatic sermon-machines which simultaneously function as altars and which, upon the insertion of a dime, will reel out a sermon no more than ten minutes long on any topic desired—all simply in order to ward off, with this din, the deadly boredom that is quietly but surely taking over religious life.

285   Naturally it is much easier and more comfortable to turn a church or a religious service into something amusing; to gamble with values which our forebears shed blood and tears to instill in us; to squander a wealth of knowledge stored up by our ancestors in the course of eighteen hundred years of tumultuous evolution, than to teach people things that must be learned by hard work, and thus to lead them to new and vaster heights.

286   There is no trick to throwing out the baby with the bathwater. And to say, "We are throwing out everything that has been built up around the figure of Christ for eighteen centuries, all the teachings, all the traditions, and will accept only the historical Jesus"— this is not much of a feat either, for as a rule the people who talk this way really have nothing to throw away in the first place. Yet frequently we hear their attitude described as "critical." Our descendants will hardly thank us if we, who are called to make the human race grow and flourish, leave behind us such fruits as a ravaged church composed of intolerable rules and shallow religious concepts which trail off into a wasteland.

287   So here we are, asking ourselves what we ought to do. Why do the sermons about the historical Jesus make no sense? Why are people more interested in attending scientific lectures than in going to church? Why is their interest focused on Darwin, Haeckel, and Büchner?[15] And why today do they not even bother to discuss

[15] Ernst Haeckel (1834-1919), German biologist, advocate of the nineteenth-century

religious questions which, in the past, people were willing to kill for? Indeed, in certain circles the discussion of religious issues is considered not only awkward but downright unseemly. Our society must be educated, we must instill in it a concern for the supreme questions, and only after all this has been done ought we to begin preaching about the so-called historical Jesus and to appeal to the sense of value that people ascribe to Christ. But this sense of value will not arise until the world has grasped the fact that Christ is not a "normal man," any more than he is an element in a world of abstract concepts totally divorced from reality. We should and must interpret Christ as he himself taught us to interpret him. The image of Christ must be restored to the idea he had of himself, namely as a prophet, a man sent by God. The position he occupies in our mental universe must be consistent with his own claims. Modern man must accept the supramundane nature of Christ, no more and no less. If we do not accept it we are no longer Christians, for we are not entitled to bear this name when we have ceased to share the views it implies. But as long as we call ourselves by Christ's name, we are morally bound to observe his teachings in all respects. We *must* believe even what seems impossible, or we will be abusing the name of Christian. This is a harsh prescription, and will be denounced as an abdication of the intellect. But once someone has taken it into his head to be a Christian, he must defend his faith against his critical reason, even at the risk of a new flowering of scholasticism. If he does not wish to do this, there is a very easy way out: he must simply give up his intention to be a Christian. Then he may call himself by any other name he chooses—a man concerned with the preservation of moral decency, or a moral philosopher bent on improving the world. But if our Christianity is to possess any substance whatever, we must once again accept unconditionally the whole of the metaphysical, conceptual universe of the first Christians. To do this will be to drive a painful thorn into our flesh, but for the sake of our title as Christians, we must. I call on everyone, and especially theologians, to remember the truth that Eduard von Hartmann hurled down at the feet of all Christians, and I implore that they hearken to his voice: "The world of

theory of the metamorphosis of species over the course of time. Ludwig Büchner (1824-1899), German materialistic philosopher.

metaphysical ideas must always remain the living fountain of feeling in religious worship, which rouses the will to ethical action. Whenever this fountain dries up, worship becomes petrified and turns into a dead, meaningless ceremony, while religious ethics wither into a dry and abstract moralizing or a sentimental phrase-mongering which holds no attaction for anyone!"

288   The mystery of a metaphysical world, a metaphysical order, of the kind that Christ taught and embodied in his own person, must be placed in center stage of the Christian religion, and must occupy its summit as the Prime Mover. Hartmann says: "*No religion whatever is possible without the premonitory depth and infinite richness of that mystery which shows a different aspect to every human being.*"

289   No religion has survived, or ever will, without mystery, to which the devotee is most intimately bound. Even modern historically oriented Christianity has its miracles, its mystery. But alas, alas, this miracle par excellence—the effect on man of the person of Christ and man's consequent conversion—is inevitably a fictive miracle in that its cause is not the real presence of Christ (*in substantia*), but only an idea that we, as subjects of cognition, have endowed with the power to motivate our actions. By a strict definition of the term "miracle," the altered conduct of somebody converted in accordance with Ritschl's view of causation cannot constitute a miracle, for the efficient cause of this conduct is that idea which predominates over the will, an idea whose reality is determined by the reality of the subject who knows it. In ordinary, unstilted scientific language this is called autosuggestion. And nowadays the concept of autosuggestion no longer falls into the category of miracle, for if it did, we would also be forced to marvel daily at the miracle of gravitation. We often hear theologians say: It is in fact the great miracle, which makes clear to us the immediate effect which Christ exercises on our lives, that a person can be totally transformed when he grasps the person of Christ. If they interpret this phenomenon in the same way as Ritschl, this would mean that the miracle in question is no greater than if a hypochondriac who has read about tuberculosis were himself to start coughing and spitting. But if they interpret it, in Christian terms, as referring to the material, substantial presence of Christ, then it is indeed a great miracle. But then why not do away with Ritschl's nomenclature too,

along with the concept of the historical Jesus,[16] which has meaning only if it is used by an adherent of Ritschl's ideas? For in this case Christ is a metaphysical figure with whom we are bound in a mystical union which raises us up out of the sensory world. And in this case, we laymen should dispense with the idea of the historical Jesus, for it now has a fixed meaning derived from Ritschl, and lends itself to no further interpretation but only to *mis*interpretation. In this case the theologian ought rather to speak in the language of Heinrich Suso, which does not lend itself to misunderstanding, or in the profound and obscure images of a Jakob Boehme. By doing so he will approach the summit of religious feeling more nearly than through the insipid phrases of progressive theology.

290   I leave it up to every man who desires to be a Christian to decide whether or not a *unio mystica* is possible. And every man who bears this name with honor will come to a positive decision, for Christ viewed himself as one who possessed both ability and desire to remain with his people "even unto the end of the world." This is a dangerous view and inevitably brings with it that peril feared by Ritschl, namely that it eliminates any possibility of distinguishing between reality and hallucination. In its train follow the entire mystical tradition, the problems of asceticism and of ecstatic knowledge, and those of the divinity of Christ and the infallibility of his teachings. Any consistent realization of the mystical idea must inevitably reintroduce debate concerning the objects of scholastic speculation, and thereby come close to the possibility of social and scientific indifference and call into question the further progress of civilization. These are all ominous, far-reaching, and bewildering possibilities which it would not occur to anyone to be concerned about if it were not for the fact that during the thousand years of the Middle Ages, mankind witnessed their reign for long periods. Anyone who wishes to hold fast to the metaphysical reality of the elements of Christian faith must realize these dangers and difficulties and must never lose sight of the fact that Christianity represents nothing less than the break with an entire world, a dehumanization of man, a "revaluation of all values" (Nietzsche). There is not one single element of civilization that can turn a profit on Christian teachings. Everything takes second place to the one great

[16] *Deleted*: The concept of personhood? Why not do away with the exact remembrance of tradition?

question, that of the inner spiritualization of the individual and the concomitant disintegration of the existing order of nature. Christ came to bring not peace but a sword, for he unleashes the conflict of the dualistic, divided will.

291   For almost two thousand years, from its birth in the theology of John until its decline in Schopenhauer, that dangerous interpretation of Christian faith which formed the foundation of the medieval world-view has fascinated the most distinguished minds. This is cause enough to doubt that it has been completely extinguished, and cause to expect that we have not yet seen the last lightning bolt flare up out of its dark reaches.

Plurimi pertransibunt, et multiplex erit scientia![17]

[17] "Many shall perish, and manifold shall be knowledge!"

APPENDIX
TO PART V

TEXTS[1]

[1] These are Jung's research notes for the lecture on Ritschl, which he preserved with the lecture MS.

From Matthew

Christ's first words to the human race:

1. Repent ye: for the kingdom of heaven is at hand. [3:2][2]

The Sermon on the Mount [Matt. 5]:

2. Blessed are the poor in spirit: for theirs is the kingdom of heaven.
3. Blessed are the pure in heart: for they shall see God.
4. Blessed are they which are persecuted for righteousness' sake: for theirs is the kingdom of heaven.
5. Rejoice, and be exceeding glad: for great is your reward in heaven.
6. Whosoever therefore shall break one of these least commandments, and shall teach men so, he shall be called the least in the kingdom of heaven: but whosoever shall do and teach them, the same shall be called great in the kingdom of heaven. For I say unto you, That except your righteousness shall exceed the righteousness of the scribes and Pharisees, ye shall in no case enter into the kingdom of heaven.
7. Thy kingdom come. [6:10]
8. Deliver us from evil. [6:13]
9. Lay not up for yourselves treasures upon earth. . . . But lay up for yourselves treasures in heaven. [6:19-20]
10. Take no thought for your life, what ye shall eat, or what ye shall drink; nor yet for your body, what ye shall put on. [6:25]
11. But seek ye first the kingdom of God, and his righteousness, etc. [6:33]
12. Strait is the gate, and narrow is the way, which leadeth unto life, and few there be that find it. [7:14]
13. Follow me; and let the dead bury their dead. [8:22].
14. (To the apostles): And as ye go, preach, saying, The kingdom of heaven is at hand. [10:7]
15. Behold, I send you forth as sheep in the midst of wolves. [10:16]
16. But beware of men. [10:17]

[1] These are Jung's research notes for the lecture on Ritschl, which he preserved with the lecture MS.
[2] The words in this text are those of John the Baptist.

17. But verily I say unto you, Ye shall not have gone over the cities of Israel, till the Son of Man be come. [10:23]
18. Whosoever therefore shall confess me before men, him will I confess also before my Father which is in heaven. [10:32]
19. Think not that I am come to send peace on earth, etc. [10:34]
20. He that loveth father or mother more than me is not worthy of me, etc. [10:37]
21. (To John the Baptist): The blind receive their sight, and the lame walk, the lepers are cleansed, and the deaf hear, the dead are raised up, and the poor have the gospel preached to them. [11:5]

Matt. 11:21ff. Miracles

22. All things are delivered unto me of my Father: and no man knoweth the Son, but the Father, etc. [11:27]
23. Take my yoke upon you, and learn of me; for I am meek and lowly in heart. [11:29]
24. Who is my mother? and who are my brethren? [12:48].
25. For verily I say unto you, That many prophets and righteous men have desired to see those things which ye see, and have not seen them; and to hear those things which ye hear, and have not heard them. [13:17]

Knowledge

26. (To the disciples): Because it is given unto you to know the mysteries of the kingdom of heaven, etc. [13:11]
27. (Reference to Isaiah): I will open my mouth in parables; I will utter things which have been kept secret from the foundation of the world. [13:35]
28. For the Son of Man shall come in the glory of his Father with his angels; and then he shall reward every man according to his works. [16:27]
29. *The Transfiguration.* [Matt. 17]
30. *Miracles*: If ye have faith as a grain of mustard seed, ye shall say unto this mountain, Remove hence to yonder place; and it shall remove; and nothing shall be impossible unto you. [17:19]
31. Take heed that ye despise not one of these little ones; for I say unto you, That in heaven their angels do always behold the face of my Father which is in heaven. [18:10]
32. So likewise shall my heavenly Father do also unto you, if ye from your hearts forgive not every one his brother his trespasses. [18:35]
33. There be eunuchs which have made themselves eunuchs for the kingdom of heaven's sake. [19:12]
34. When his disciples heard it, they were exceedingly amazed, saying,

Who then can be saved? But Jesus beheld them, and said unto them, With men this is impossible; but with God all things are possible. [19:25-26]

35. Verily I say unto you, That ye which have followed me, in the regeneration when the Son of Man shall sit in the throne of his glory, ye also shall sit upon twelve thrones, etc. [19:28]

36. And every one that hath forsaken houses, or brethren, or sisters, or father, or mother, or wife, or children, or lands, for my name's sake, shall receive an hundredfold, and shall inherit everlasting life. [19:29]

37. *Prophecy concerning the imminent end of the world.* [Matt. 24]

38. Therefore be ye also ready: for in such an hour as ye think not the Son of Man cometh. [24:44]

39. Thinkest thou that I cannot now pray to my Father, and he shall presently give me more than twelve legions of angels? [26:53]

40. Nevertheless I say unto you: Hereafter shall ye see the Son of Man sitting on the right hand of power, and coming in the clouds of heaven. [26:64]

Mark

41. The time is fulfilled, and the kingdom of God is at hand: repent ye, and believe the gospel. [1:15]

Luke

42. They that are whole need not a physician; but they that are sick. I came not to call the righteous, but sinners to repentance. [5:31-32]

43. Rejoice ye in that day, and leap for joy: for behold, your reward is great in heaven. [6:23]

44. For with the same measure that ye mete withal it shall be measured to you again. [6:38]

45. For whosoever shall be ashamed of me and of my words, of him shall the Son of Man be ashamed, when he shall come in his own glory, and in his Father's, and of the holy angel. [9:26]

46. I beheld Satan as lightning fall from heaven. [10:18]

47. Notwithstanding in this rejoice not, that the spirits are subject unto you: but rather rejoice, because your names are written in heaven. [10:20]

48. Blessed are the eyes which see the things that ye see, etc. [10:23]

49. Woe unto thee, Chorazin, etc. [10:13ff.]

50. The *Our Father.* Give us this day our daily bread. [11:13]

51. Woe unto you, lawyers! for ye have taken away the key of knowledge: ye entered not in yourselves, and them that were entering in ye hindered. [11:52]

52. Thou fool, this night thy soul shall be required of thee: then whose shall those things be, which thou hast provided? [12:20]

53. I am come to send fire on the earth; and what will I, if it be already kindled? [12:49]

54. Suppose ye that I am come to give peace on earth? I tell you, Nay; but rather division: For from henceforth there shall be five in one house divided, three against two, and two against three. The father shall be divided against the son, and the son against the father, etc. [12:51-53]

55. If any man come to me, and hate not his father, and mother, and wife, and children, and brethren, and sisters, yea, and his own life also, he cannot be my disciple. [14:26]

Appearances after death. [Luke 24]

Hartmann, Wundt, Ritschl / Evolut. optima.

Ritschl. Metaphysics and religion.
Luthardt's[3] opinion, page 1.
Luther[4] page 4. Throwing out the baby with the bathwater.
        page 14. Possible metaphysical purpose of the world.

Ritschl is forced to combat people who still think of God as the absolute and speculate on his necessary properties.
page 42. Interpretation of the Holy Spirit as the motive force of ethical action. The sense of value attached to the memory is erroneously equated with a real sensation.
page 45. One can act upon others only within the sensory realm. Thus only subjective images in memory to which our sense of value attributes activity and reality, can serve as the motivation for ethical action. Thence follows the proof of the reality of God, since tradition has inculcated us with its remembered value.

[3] Christoph Ernst Luthardt (1823-1902), Lutheran theologian, author of *Apologie des Christentums* (1864-1880).
[4] Martin Luther (1483-1546), father of the Reformation in Germany. The references here could not be traced.

INDEX

INDEX

A

absolute, as One, 77

absorption, inorganic principle of, 80

abstraction, as source of erroneous conclusions, 68

Academy, French, 42

actio in distans (long-range effect), 40ff.

"active imagination," a form of meditation used by Jung, xxiv

activity: life as highest, 85; as root of human nature, 85. *See also* energy, passive and active

actus purus, in Ritschl's thought, 97, 101

adhesion, inorganic principle of, 80

Adler, Gerhard, xxi*n*

Aether, 11*n*. *See also* ether

affinity, inorganic principle of, 80

Aksakov, Alexander, 35

alchemy, xxiv

Alsace-Lorraine, 105

America, 69

angel, miracle of, at Bethesda, 98

archetype, foreshadowing of concept of, xxi

argumentum ad hominem, 74

argumentum ad rem, 74

Ariadne, 18

Aristotle, (quote) 87, (quote) 98

Armenia, persecution of, 10

Athens, as educational ideal, 56

atom, definition of, 15f.

atomic theory, 11, 15

Austral Islands (French Polynesia), 76*n*

"authorities," scholarly, 7f.

B

Barnes, Jonathan, 87*n*

Barth, Karl, xxiii

Basel, 3, 37, 53, 59, 71*n*

Basel University, 5*n*; and the Zofingia fraternity, xiii

Bastian, Henry Charlton, 16

Bauer, E., xvi*n*

Berlin, 6, 71*n*

Berlin University, 6

Bernoulli, Carl Albrecht, 75*n*; his novel *Lucas Heland*, (quote) 74-75

Bethesda, *see* angel

Bible, miraculous elements of, 43; Biblical sayings of Jesus, xxiii. *See also* under individual books; *Jerusalem Bible*

Binzer, August, 47*n*

Birkhäuser, Kaspar, xv*n*

Blücher, Gebhard Leberecht von, 42*n*, (quote) 54

Boehme, Jakob, xxii, 110; and the opposites, (quote) 79, (quote) 83

Brenner, 55

"Breo" pub, xiv

Breslau, 84*n*

British Association, 36

Büchner, Ludwig, 36, 44, 107, 108*n*

Buddha, xxiii, 96f.

Burckhardt, Abel, 53

Burckhardt, Jakob, 53*n*

Burdach, Karl Friedrich, (quote) 29, (quote) 30

Burschenschaften (German student associations), xv

Byron, George Gordon, Lord, 86

C

capillarity, inorganic principle of, 80

careerism, 10

categorical imperative, xx, 66, 67*n*, 68*n*

categories, a priori, 68

cathode rays, 24*n*